Treatise on the Love of God
Treatise on the Priesthood

SAINT JOHN OF AVILA

TREATISE ON THE LOVE OF GOD
&
TREATISE ON THE PRIESTHOOD

New York – 2012

Cover Design
    © IVE Press

Cover Art
    © IVE Press

Text
    © IVE Press, New York
    Institute of the Incarnate Word, Inc.
    All rights reserved

Manufactured in the United States of America.

IVE Press
    113 East 117th Street
    New York, NY 10035

    Ph. (646) 470-9590
    Fax (855) 483-2665

    Email orders@ivepress.org
    http:// www.ivepress.com

    ISBN 1-933871-47-4
    ISBN 978-1-933871-47-9

Library of Congress Control Number: 2011903652

    Printed in the United States of America ∞

TABLE OF CONTENTS

Treatise on the Love of God 9
   1. God Loves Us with the Love of a Father, Mother and Spouse 11
   2. All Things Speak to Us of the Love of God. 13
   3. Christ, the Supreme Expression of the Love that God has for Us 14
   4. Christ Loves Us 14
   5. The Mystery of Christ 15
   6. Christ, Head of the Mystical Body 16
   7. The Beauty of the Soul of Christ 17
   8. Our Predestination in Christ 18
   9. The Foundation of the Love that Christ has for Us 19
   10. The Love of Christ is an Endless Abyss 22
   11. The Zeal of the Heart of Jesus Surpasses the Zeal of the Saints 23
   12. Christ is Wedded to the Church 24
   13. Who Will Not Return Love to Christ? 25
   14. The Madness of the Cross 26
   15. Confidence in Christ 29
   16. Christ is Still Present 32

Treatise on the Priesthood 33
1. The Reason for the Ministerial Priesthood.......................... 35
Being a Priest as a Gift of God *35*
The Opinion of the People of God *36*
Mary and the Priestly Ministry *37*
In the Mystery of Christ *38*
The Dignity of Serving *39*
Priestly Sanctity: Living What We Are *40*
Facing God and Men: Prayer and Sacrifice *41*
2. Prayer as a Priestly Task.. 42
Responsibility for All Humanity *42*
Prayer of Mediation *43*
In Divine Intimacy *45*
The Priestly Sentiments of Christ *46*
Sensitivity to the Interests of God and the Problems of Men *47*
Lack of Priestly Prayer *49*
3. Sacrifice: Being a Victim with Christ the Priest 50
Mediating Sacrifice *50*
Intimacy with Christ *51*
Sign of Christ the Victim *53*
The Physiognomy of Christ *54*
Priestly Chastity *55*
In the Old Law *56*
Apostolic Inheritance *57*
The Thought of the Fathers *58*
The Testimony of the Saints *61*
Like the Baptist and St. Peter *62*
Imitation of the Virgin Mary *63*
Spirit of Sacrifice *64*
Purity of Heart *64*
Priestly Humility *65*
4. Renewal of the Priesthood 66
The Call to Renewal *66*
The Priest as a Sign of Christ *68*
To Crucify Christ Again? *69*
The Sense of Sin *70*
Sin in the Priest *71*
Loss of the Fear of God *73*
A Possible Failure *74*

  Suffering in Union with Christ *75*
  The Sorrow of the Church *76*
  Lack of a Sense of the Church *77*
  A Distressing Situation *79*
 5. Parish Priests 79
  The Dignity and Sanctity of the Pastor *79*
  Sanctification in the Ministry *80*
  Preaching and Study *81*
  Orientation and Direction *82*
 6. Confessors 83
  The Ministry of Confession *83*
  Renewal *84*
  The Root of the Evil *85*
  Conciliar Doctrine *86*
  Unfulfilled Conciliar Decrees *87*
 7. Preachers 87
  Proclamation of the Word *87*
  Christ, the Word of God *88*
  The Word Now Present in the Church *88*

Bull of Canonization **91**

  Introduction *93*
  The consciousness of priestly dignity and the reform of customs,
  motives for canonization *93*
 1. The Life of Saint John of Avila 94
  Studies and preparation to go to Mexico *94*
  Apostolic mission in Andalucía *95*
  He leaves the Inquisition, innocent and penetrated by the "Mystery
  of Christ" *95*
  Córdoba and Granada; teacher of priests and of saints *96*
  Foundation of the University of Baeza *96*
  Saint John of Ávila and Saint Ignatius of Loyola *97*
  His last years in Montilla *97*
  Writer and spiritual director *97*
  He died serenely on the 10th of May of 1569 .... *98*
 2. The Holiness of Saint John of Ávila 98
  Faithful image of Saint Paul *98*
  Projects of reform sent to the Council of Trent *99*
  Friend of all and Teacher of Saints *99*

  Mystery of Christ: "Flesh, Cross, Eucharist" *99*
  The topic of priesthood in his writings *100*
  Teacher of Virtues *100*
 3. Following the Death of Saint John of Avila 101
  Beatification, 15th of April of 1894 .... *101*
  Towards the equipollent canonization *101*
  Heroic virtues and uninterrupted cult *102*
  The last stage *102*
  31st of May of 1970, Solemn canonization *102*

Canonization of Blessed John of Avila 105

Notes 121

Treatise on the Love of God

✠

The Mystery of Christ the Priest

God's Love for Man

1.

God Loves Us with the Love of a Father, Mother and Spouse

What most moves the human heart to love God is to consider deeply the love that God the Father and His Most Blessed Son, our Savior, have for us.

The heart is moved by love more than it benefits from it; for one who gives a benefit to another gives something that he has, but one who loves gives himself along with what he has, and there remains nothing more to give.

Then let us now see, O Lord, if You love us; and if it is thus that You love us, just how great Your love is for us.

Fathers love their children very much. Is it then our good fortune that You love us as a Father? We have not entered into the bosom of Your heart to see this, but Your Only-Begotten Son, who descended from Your bosom (Jn 1), brought us signs of that love, and He commanded us to call you *Father* (Mt 6:9) on account of the greatness of the love that You have for us. Above all, He told us that we should *call no man on earth father*, because You alone are our Father (Mt 23:9). For just as You alone are good, by the eminence of Your sovereign goodness, thus You alone are Father; and You are Father in such a way, and You do such things for us, that in comparison to Your paternal heart, there is no one else who can be called such.

Your prophet understood this well when he said, *For my father and my mother have forsaken me, but the Lord will take me up* (Ps 26:10)[a].

---

[a] In certain texts, there is a fair amount of difference between the modern RSV translation and the older, Douay-Rheims Catholic Bible, which is the English translation of the Latin Vulgate (which is most likely what St. John of Avila

You Yourself wished to be compared to parents, saying through Isaiah, *Can a woman forget the child at her breast, that she should have no compassion on the son of her womb? Even though these may forget, yet I will not forget you. Behold, I have graven you on the palms of my hands; your walls are continually before Me* (Is 49:15-16). And because among birds, the eagle is most well known in loving its offspring, You wished to draw an analogy between the greatness of Your love and that love of the eagle, by saying, *Like an eagle that stirs up its nest, that flutters over its young, spreading out its wings, catching them, bearing them on its pinions* (Dt 32:11).

This love is above the love of a wife, concerning which Genesis 2:4 says, *Therefore a man leaves his father and his mother and cleaves to his wife, and they become one flesh.* But Your love surpasses this, for, according to what You say through Jeremiah (3:1ff): *If a man divorces his wife and she goes from him and becomes another man's wife, will he return to her? Would not that land be greatly polluted? You have played the harlot with many lovers; nevertheless, return to Me, says the Lord, and I will receive thee.*[b]

---

would have used as his biblical source). For example, the RSV version differs slightly from the Douay-Rheims in the numbering of Psalms. This one would be Psalm 27 in the RSV, though it appears as Psalm 26 in the Douay-Rheims version and the Latin Vulgate.

[b] When there are such apparent differences in a particular text as mentioned above, we will give the Douay-Rheims translation of the text, in order to better understand St. John of Avila's meaning. We will also give the original text from the RSV translation in a footnote, such as follows:

If a man divorces his wife and she goes from him and becomes another man's wife, will he return to her? Would not that land be greatly polluted? You have played the harlot with many lovers; and would you return to me? says the LORD.

2.

All Things Speak to Us of the Love of God.

And if you are still incredulous regarding this love, look at all the benefits that God has provided for you, for all these are pledges and a witness of love.

Consider all the benefits there are, and you will find that all the creatures in heaven and on earth, all the parts and senses in your body, and all the hours and moments in which you live your life—that all of these are benefits provided by the Lord.

Consider also how many good inspirations you have received and how many goods you have had in this life; from how many sins He has freed you and how many sicknesses and disasters you could have fallen into, if He had not delivered you from them. All these things are signs and tokens of His love.

Even the scourges and tribulations themselves that He sent to you are evidences of love, for they are samples of the heart of that Father who chastises every son whom He receives (Heb 12:6), in order to correct him and wake him up, to cleanse him and preserve him in every good gift.

Finally, cast your eyes on the whole of this world, all of which He made on account of His love for you; and the whole of it, and all the things there are in it—they all preach love, demand love, and signify love.

3.

Christ, the Supreme Expression of the Love that God has for Us

And should you be deaf to all these things, that is no reason for you to be so in regards to the appeals that the Savior makes to you in the Gospel, *For God so loved the world that He gave his only Son, that whoever believes in Him should not perish, but have eternal life* (Jn 3:16).

All these things are signs of love, and there is one that is greater than all the rest, according to His evangelist Saint John, who is so great a lover of God and so beloved by God, who writes this, *In this the love of God was made manifest among us, that God sent His only Son into the world, so that we might live through Him* (1 Jn 4:9). And this gift, along with all the others, are signs of the love that God has for us, and they are like flashes of lightning that strike here from that scorching fire of love.

O how much greater must be that hidden fire, since the sparks of it are so great! O tremendous love! O gracious love! Oh love so worthy of being repaid by love! *Grant us*, O Lord, *the power to comprehend with all the saints what is the breadth and length and height and depth of that love* (Eph 3:18) so that our whole heart may be wounded and conquered by Your love.

4.

Christ Loves Us

But let us see how great the love was that the Son, whom You gave to us, had toward us.. There is no language that could explain it. As St. Paul says, *the love of Christ surpasses all knowledge* (Eph

3:19), even the knowledge of the angels, because none of them will succeed in knowing it.

Some ignorant and coarse men have not come to the realization of this love. For them, love is born from the goodness and perfection found in the thing loved (because the true object of such love is the goodness and perfection of things), and given that man is a creature that is so lowly and imperfect, in regards to both his body and his soul, being a vessel of evil, with what kind of love could such a miserable creature be loved, considering especially the fact that the divine Lover is not blind, nor impassioned, nor the least capricious. For where there is neither blindness nor passion in the one who loves, and where the thing that is to be loved is so ugly and miserable, what kind of love will one be able to have for it?

But this is not the kind of reckoning that should be made in order to measure this love, for the love of Christ is not born from the perfection that is found in us, but from that which He has, which mirrors that of His Eternal Father.

5.

The Mystery of Christ

As a result (taking up the business of the first principles), you should consider the inestimable greatness of the graces that were granted by the Most Holy Trinity to that Most Holy Humanity of Christ in the instant of His conception (Col 2:3-9).

For there were three graces granted to His Humanity which are so great that each of them in its own way is infinite. These are, namely, the grace of the divine union, the universal grace that was given Him as Head of the whole Church, and the essential grace of His soul.

First, the Divine being itself was given to that sacred Humanity, joining with it and uniting it with the Divine Person. Indeed, the Divine being was given to that Humanity in such way that we can truly say that this man is God and the Son of God, and He is to be adored in heaven and on earth as God.

This grace is already seen to be infinite by the gift that is given in it (which is the greatest thing that possibly can be given, since God is given in it), and by the manner in which it is given, which is in the most intimate way possible, that is, by way of personal union.

6.

Christ, Head of the Mystical Body

Likewise, it was given to this new man that He would be universal Father and Head of all mankind, in order that, as their spiritual Head, His virtue would influence all of them (Col 1:18; 2:9).

Thus, as God, He is equal to the Eternal Father, and as man, He is principle and Head of all mankind. In conformity with this preeminence, an infinite grace is given to Him in order that all men might receive it from Him, as from a fount of grace and a sea of holiness (Jn 1:16). This is true not only because He is greater than all men, but because He is the sanctifier of all men, He is so to speak, a dye of holiness from which all those who are to become saints must receive their color and luster.

This grace is also infinite because it is for the whole human race, which does not have a determined number of persons, but is able, in so far as it is concerned, to be increased to infinity. And for all those who are multiplied in the human race, there are merits and grace in the blessed soul of Jesus Christ.

7.

The Beauty of the Soul of Christ

Finally, another absolutely singular grace is given to Him for the sanctification and perfection of His own life. This also can be called infinite, because it has all that pertains to the being and perfection of grace, and there is nothing that can be added.

In addition to all this, there were given to Him at that moment all the graces *gratia data*, for performing as many miracles and marvels as He wished. And they all were given to Him in the highest degree and in the greatest perfection.

For this is the beautiful *flower* of loveliness where the white dove of the *Holy Spirit* rested, and sheltered it with His outstretched wings and completely spread over it all virtue and grace (Is 11:2).

This is the *chosen vessel* which is filled with the river of all graces, with all its floods and tides, without a single drop remaining that does not enter into Him (cf Jn 1).

Here God did all that He could do and gave all that He could give, because here He produced the ultimate instance of power and grace, giving everything that was possible to that most happy soul at the moment that it was created.

And above all that, there was given to His soul in that same moment, that it saw then the divine essence and knew clearly the majesty and glory of the Word with whom it was united. And, thus seeing, it was blessed and filled with as much glory as it now has at the right hand of the Father.

8.

Our Predestination in Christ

If this gift, which is so tremendous, attracts your admiration, join to it this other marvelous circumstance that accompanies it. This, the fact that all this was given Him as pure grace, before all meriting, before that blessed soul could have performed any meritorious work by which it could have deserved it.

All of this was done at once, the creating of it and the endowing of it with all these graces. And this was done for no other reason than that the Lord, in this way, wished to exalt it, and to extend His hands and largess toward it, and thus magnify His grace.

For this reason, Saint Augustine calls Jesus Christ *a paragon and example of grace.* For just as great writers and painters are accustomed to place some samples of their labors in their work place, in which, employing all their know-how, they want to be recognized, and they display all their power so that everybody may see how great is their achievement, so likewise this infinite goodness and largess of God determined to raise up a new creature and bestow on it all its magnificence and grace, so that by this work the heavens and the earth might recognize His greatness.

King Ahasuerus held a marvelous banquet for his whole kingdom. God made a greater and more marvelous banquet for this humanity to which He was espoused, so that all the celestial and earthly creatures might know by it the largess and divine nobility of His kindness, which extended to such things.

O see how great and admirable this gift is, and see how happy that blessed soul has been to whom God wished to grant such a grace—and have no envy, but rather happiness, since the grace that He received was not only received for Himself, but also for you.

In His name those words of Job were written, *If I have eaten my morsel alone, and the fatherless hath not eaten thereof. For from my infancy mercy grew up with me, and it came out with me from my mother's womb* (31:17-18)[c]. So He did not eat His morsel alone, but shared it beforehand with the pilgrims.

He received what He received as our true *Head*, and did so not only for Himself, but for His members also.

9.

The Foundation of the Love that Christ has for Us

Now let us move on and see what comes to us from such great riches as these.

O speak to me regarding this holy soul, how in that happy moment when it was created, He would open His eyes and would see Himself such as you have heard, and would know from whose hands so much good has come to Him, and speak about how He who is born a king, and does not gain His kingship with a lance, finds Himself in the principality of all the creatures and saw kneeling before Himself all the hierarchies of heaven, which in that happy moment adored Him, as St. Paul says (Heb 1:6). Tell me, if it is possible, with what love such a soul as this would love which has been glorified in this way. With what desire would it covet something that would be offered to it, with which it could please and serve such a Giver? Are there any tongues of the cherubim and seraphim that can tell us this?

---

[c] This appears to be closer to the Douay-Rheims translation. The RSV says, *or have eaten my morsel alone, and the fatherless has not eaten of it (for from his youth I reared him as a father, and from his mother's womb I guided him).*

Then let us add more. To one with such great desire, it was made known that the will of God was that He should desire to save the human race, which was lost through the fault of a man, and that this blessed Son has been entrusted with this task, on account of His honor and obedience; and He took this glorious venture to heart, and He would not rest until it would come to its completion.

And because it is the *modus operandi* of all causes and creatures to work on account of love (because all of them work for some end that they desire, the love of which is conceived in their hearts), and therefore, because He had to take upon Himself this work of the redemption of men—He who loved them with so much love and desire, who on account of love desired to see them healed and reestablished in their own glory—so He took upon Himself to do and to suffer whatever was necessary to accomplish this end.

Tell me, now, once that soul understood this, and being so desirous of pleasing the Eternal Father, with what kind of love would it turn towards men to love them and to embrace them, because of that obedience to the Father?

We see that when an artillery shot fires a cannon ball with a great deal of gunpowder and force, and the cannon ball rebounds from its target, it does so with much greater force, the greater the ferocity of its original propulsion.

So, if that love of Christ's soul toward God carried such tremendous force (because the gunpowder of grace that was driving it was infinite), and after having gone directly to wound the heart of the Father, it rebounds from there to the love of men, then with how much force and joy will it not turn upon them in order to love them and renew them? There is neither language nor created power that can signify this.

This is that force that the prophet referred to when he said, *and like a strong man runs its course with joy. Its rising is from the end of the heavens, and its circuit to the end of them; and there is nothing hid from its heat* (Ps 19:5-6). O love divine that went forth from God and descended upon man and returned to God! (Jn 16:28). For You did not love man for man's sake, but for God's. And in such a way did You love man, that, whoever considers this love, *cannot hide from Your love* because You employ force on our hearts, as your Apostle puts it, *The charity of Christ compels us* (2 Cor 5:14).

This is whom Your holy Church referred to in the Song of Songs (2:8-9): *Behold, He comes, leaping upon the mountains, bounding over the hills. My Beloved is like a gazelle, or a young stag,* according to the agility that He has. The prophet Isaiah meant this same thing (42:4) when he said, *He will not fail or be discouraged till He has established justice in the earth; and the coastlands wait for His law*. From this text were born those words that are so spirited which said, *I will not give sleep to my eyes or slumber to my eyelids, until I find a place for the Lord, a dwelling place for the Mighty One of Jacob* (Ps 132:4-5).

If one wants to know the source and origin of Christ's love toward men, this is it. For the cause of this love is neither the virtue, nor the kindness, nor the beauty of man, but rather Christ's virtues, His gratitude, His grace and his indescribable charity toward God.

This is what those words mean that He spoke at the Last Supper, *so that the world may know that I love the Father. Rise, let us go hence* (Jn 14:31). But where does he go? To die for men on the cross.

So my soul, examine here the cause of this great love. The more the brilliance of the sun burns, so much the stronger are the beams that are reflected from it. The direct beams of that divine Son were going to be given to the heart of God; from thence, they were reflected onto men. So if the beams are so strong, how much more will His brilliance burn?

10.

The Love of Christ is an Endless Abyss

Even the angels do not reach an understanding of how great this fire is, nor to what heights His power reaches.

There is no limit to which His death and cross could arrive. For it was the same thing that they should send Him to suffer one death, as if they had sent Him to suffer thousands of deaths, for He had sufficient love for all of them. And if what they sent Him to suffer for all mankind, they sent Him to suffer for each one of them, He was thus doing for each one what He was doing for all. And if His hanging those three hours on the cross needed to be prolonged until the Day of Judgment, He had love for all that, if it was necessary for us, so be it.

Thus He loved us much more than what He suffered for us, so that much greater love remained pent up in His heart than was shown here externally in His wounds.

It is worth noting that He willed that the Holy Spirit should write, not without great mystery, that, among other peculiarities of Solomon's temple, the windows of the temple were shaped like arrow slits, so that inside they were larger than they seemed on the outside (1 Kgs 6:4). O Divine love! How much greater You are than You appear! You appear great here from the outside, because Your many injuries, so many wounds and lashes, undoubtedly preach to us a great love; but they do not speak of the whole nobility that it has, because it is greater there inside than it appears from the outside. This is but a spark that comes forth from that fire, a branch that comes forth from this tree, a creek that is born from that ocean of immense love. This is the greatest sign that can exist of love, *He lays down his life for his friends* (Jn 15:13), but it is a sign and not an equality.

So if I owe so much to You for what You did for me, how much more will I owe You for what You wanted to do? If so great is the public deed that the eyes of all see, how much greater will be what only the eyes of God see? O ocean of love! O bottomless abyss full of love! Who now will doubt Christ's love? Who will not hold himself to be the richest one in the world, since he is loved by such a Lord?

I beseech You, my Lord, by the heart of compassion that moved You to give such a gift, give me eyes and a heart so that I may feel and know this love, so that I may always glory in Your mercies and may sing your praises all my days.

11.

The Zeal of the Heart of Jesus Surpasses the Zeal of the Saints

If you desire, my soul, to conjecture something about the love of Christ, of the desire that He had to suffer for you, stop to think about the nobility of the desire that the saints had to suffer for God's sake, and in this way you will understand the desire that this Saint of all saints had, for He exceeds them as much in holiness and grace as the light of the sun exceeds the light of the stars, and much more.

See the desire of that blessed apostle, St. Andrew, who, seeing the cross on which he was to die, paid gallant compliments to it as one would to a very dear wife and begged it to be as happy with him as he was pleased with it.

And I come to another, higher kind of martyrdom, and to another new way of desiring, which was that of St. Paul, who, all the kinds of suffering together seeming to him too small to satisfy his desire, came to such a desire of love that he desired the sensible pains themselves of Hell for the honor of God and for the salvation of men: *For I could wish*, he says, *that I myself were anathema from Christ for my brethren's sake* (Rm 9:3). He desired in this to be separated from Christ as regards the participation in glory (although not as regards love and grace), as St. John Chrysostom says.

So, my soul, now take wings and rise up from this rung to the soul and heart of Christ, and see that if this holy Apostle, having but a drop of grace, had so great a love for men that he truly wanted to endure the pains of Hell for them, how much greater will be Christ's desires, since so much the greater was his grace and charity?

What else did You want to suggest to us in those words where You said, *I have a baptism to be baptized with; and how I am constrained until it is accomplished!* (Lk 12:50). Because Your desire to see Yourself already dyed in Your blood by force of the pains suffered for us was so great, every hour that this was deferred seemed to You a thousand years on account of the nobility of the love. And from this fact there was born that glorious celebration of the Palms, which You wanted to take place when You were going forth to suffer, in order to teach to the world the joy of Your Heart, when, surrounded thus by roses and flowers, You wished to go to the nuptial bed of the cross. Since the celebration that You willed to take place along Your path is so great, it does not seem, Lord, as if You are going to the cross, but to a wedding feast.

12.

Christ is Wedded to the Church

So go forth now, *daughters of Zion*, devout souls and lovers of Christ, *and behold King Solomon, with the crown with which his mother crowned him on the day of his wedding, on the day of the gladness of his heart* (Sng 3:11).

Lord, do I not come upon another garland that your mother, the synagogue, made for You, on that Friday of the Cross, made not of roses but of thorns, to torment Your head? Then, how will this celebration and the *gladness of Your Heart* be named? Perchance do these thorns not hurt You? Yes, to be sure, and hurt You more than any other man, because Your sensitivity was so much greater. But because of the greatness of the love You had for us, You were focusing not on Your pain, but on our healing, not on Your wounds, but on the medicine for our sick souls.

If *seven years of servitude* for the sake of wedding the beautiful Rachel seemed so little to the Patriarch Jacob *because of the love he had for her* (Gen 29:20), what did one day on the cross seem to You in order to wed the Church and make her so beautiful, *without spot or wrinkle or any such thing* (Eph 5:27).

This love makes You die so willingly; it intoxicated You to such a degree, that it caused You to be stripped naked and hung upon a cross and made a mockery of by the world. You are like Noah who planted a vineyard and drank such an abundance of its wine, that intoxicated by this powerful wine, You fell asleep on the cross and endured such humiliations on it that Your own children jeered at You and made a mockery of You.

13.

Who Will Not Return Love to Christ?

O marvelous love that lowered itself to such an extreme! And what astounding blindness of men, who took occasion here for disbelief in You, when they should have taken this occasion to love You more!

Tell me, O Most Sweet Lover! If this one spark alone that You showed us here, from the outside, was so frightening to men that it became a scandal for the Jews and madness for the gentiles, what would happen if You could give them another sample, one that that would manifest the whole nobility of Your love?

So if this sample alone, which is minor, causes the wicked man to lose his senses and his vision in the midst of the brilliance of the light, what will happen to Your true children and friends, who have truly believed in and known Your love?

This is what causes them to go out of themselves and to be astonished, when, pulled into the secret of Your heart, You reveal these secrets and enable them to experience them. From this is born the dissolution and burning of entrails, from this the desiring of torments, from this the rejoicing in tribulations (Col 1:24), from this the feeling of refreshment on the grills and in walking over the embers as if over roses, from here the desiring of tortures as if of banquets, and the rejoicing in what everybody is afraid of, and the embracing of what the world detests, and seeking *the abominations of Egypt to sacrifice them to God* (cf Ex 8:26).

"The soul," says St. Ambrose, "that is espoused to Jesus Christ, and is voluntarily joined with Him on the bed of the cross, considers nothing to be more glorious than wearing on his person the insignias and livery of the Crucified One."

14.

The Madness of the Cross

Thus, My Beloved, how will I ever repay this love to You? This alone is worthy of reward, that blood should be rewarded with blood.

So with that blood which Moses used to consummate the covenant between God and his people (which was a figure of this one), part was sprinkled on the altar, and part on the people, reconciling the people with God (Heb 9:19). That which is sprinkled on the altar is to placate God, and that which splashes on the heads of the people is to obligate the people.

O Most Sweet Lord! I recognize this obligation. Do not allow me to escape from this obligation. O let me see myself dyed with that blood and nailed to that cross.

O cross, make space for me and receive my body, and let that of my Lord go! Expand, oh crown, so that I can put my head there! Leave, oh nails, those innocent hands, and pierce my heart, and wound it with compassion and love! *For to this end*, says Your Apostle, *Christ died and returned to life, so that He might be Lord of both the dead and the living* (Rm 14:9), and not with threats and punishments, but with works of love. Count me among those that You will command, whether I am alive or dead, and may I see myself held captive under the dominion of Your love.

O, *what a wonderful way of fighting the Lord has adopted*, says that holy prophecy! (Jgs 5:8). For it is no longer by a deluge, nor with fire from heaven, but with the sweet talk of peace and love He has conquered hearts; not by killing, but by dying; not by spilling blood, but by offering His own for all on the cross.

O wonderful new power! What You did not do from Heaven served by angels, You did from the cross accompanied by thieves! O hurried and violent robber! What sword will be so strong, what bow so sturdy and well fitted, that it could penetrate a fine diamond? Yet the force of Your love has torn infinite diamonds to pieces. You have broken the hardness of our hearts. You have inflamed the whole world with Your love. You Yourself said to a prophet, *all the earth will be scorched with the fire of My love*. And in your Gospel You said, *I came to cast fire upon the earth, and would that it were already kindled!* (Lk12:49)

Well did that holy prophet understand the power of this coming and of this fire when he cried out saying, *O that Thou wouldst rend the heavens and come down! ... The waters would burn like fire* (Is 64:1-2[d]).

O sweet fire! O sweet love! O sweet flame! O sweet wounds which thus kindle hearts frozen more than snow, and converts them into love!

This is the principal aim of Your coming: to fill up the world with your love, and, as the prophet says, *You visited the earth and intoxicated it with love, and thus You multiplied its riches with such a lineage of love* (Ps 65:9).

Visiting the earth, You intoxicated earthly hearts. O most loving Lord, most gentle, most benign, most beautiful, most merciful! You intoxicate our hearts with that wine, set them afire with that fire, wound them with that arrow of Your love.

What does this cross lack to be a spiritual crossbow, since it wounds hearts in this way? The crossbow is made of wood, has a cord stretched across it and a notch half way down it, where it raises the cocked string to shoot the arrow with ferocity to make the wound greater.

This holy cross is the wood, and that body extended on it and the arms stretched out is the cord. And the hole in its side is the notch where the arrow of love is placed, in order to go forth from there to wound the heart. The crossbow has been discharged and my heart is wounded! Now let everyone know that I have a wounded heart. My heart, how will you take shelter? There is no remedy to cure you except to die.

When I see, my good Jesus, how the tip of the spear comes out of Your side, that spear becomes an arrow of love that pene-

---

[d] This quotation, particularly Is 64:2, is more similar to the Douay-Rheims translation. The RSV translation says, *O that thou wouldst rend the heavens and come down, ...as when fire kindles brushwood and the fire causes water to boil....*

trates and wounds my heart in such a way that there is no part of it that it does not penetrate.

What have You done, sweet Love? What have You desired to do in my heart? I came here to be healed, and I have been wounded! I came in order that You should teach me to live, and you make me insane! Oh most wise insanity, may I never see myself without You!

Not only the cross, but the figure itself that it has on it gently calls us to love. The head is leaning to hear us and gives us kisses of peace, with which You invite the guilty. The arms are outstretched to embrace us. The hands are pierced to give us Your goods, the side is opened to receive us into your bowels, the feet are nailed to hold onto us and never allow You to be separated from us.

So, Lord, looking at You on the cross, all that my eyes see, everything invites me to love: the wood, the figure and the mystery, the wounds of Your body, and above all, love within cries out that I love You and that my heart will never forget You.

For, how will I ever forget You? *If I forget you,*—oh Good Jesus!—*let my right hand wither! Let my tongue cleave to the roof of my mouth, if I do not remember you, if I do not set you above my highest joy!* (Ps 137:5-6)

15.

Confidence in Christ

See, then, my soul, the reason professed for the love that Christ has for us. For this love is not born from looking at what exists in man, but from looking at God and from the desire that one has to fulfill his holy will.

Well, by this same path you will be able to understand from whence come so many benefits and promises that God has made man, so that, from this, your hope may be strengthened, seeing that it has been built upon such firm foundations.

You must understand, then, that just as the reason that Christ loved man is not man, but God, so likewise the means by which God has promised so many goods to man is not man, but Christ. The reason the Son loves us is because the Father ordered Him to do so, and the reason the Father favors us is because the Son asks Him and merits it.

These are those supercelestial planets by whose marvelous influence the Church is governed and all the effects of graces are communicated to the world.

How firm are the buttresses of our love! And those of our hope are not less so. You love us, good Jesus, because Your Father ordered You to love us, and Your Father excuses us because You beg him to do it. Your looking at His Heart and Will results in Your loving me, because Your obedience thus demands it. And from His looking at Your sufferings and wounds proceeds my pardon and health, because thus do Your merits ask for these. Look always, Father and Son, always look unceasingly, for thus is my health achieved!

O vista of sovereign power! O marvelous super-celestial planets from whence come the rays of divine grace with such certainty! When will such a Son ever disobey? When will such a Father ever not look? So if the Son obeys, who will not be loved? And if the Father looks, who will not be pardoned? Upon a sigh from that maiden Achsah before her father Caleb, the pious father gave her whatever she asked of him (Jos 15:18ff). Then, upon the sighs and tears of such a Son, what could be refused to Him?

Thus, when will my remedy ever be lacking, if I will seek it? When will my merits ever be exhausted, since they are Yours? When will the mire of my sins smell so bad, but that the sacrifice of Your passion does not smell more mildly; its beauty being so great that all the sins of the world together are but a speck to spoil it, like a tiny mole on a very beautiful face?

So, my weak and distrustful soul, which in so many anxieties fails to trust in God, why do your faults and the absence of your merits make you lose heart?

See that this concern does not rest on you alone, but on Christ. It's not principally your merits alone which have to save you, but those of the Savior. For if the demerit of that first man so long ago was enough to condemn you (Rm 5:18), much more will Christ's merits suffice for saving you. He is the buttress of your hope not you.

The first earthly man was the origin of your fall; the second Celestial One is the origin and end of your remedy (1 Cor 15:47). Work so as to be joined to Him by faith and love (Jn 15:9), just as you are united to the former by the tie of kinship. For if you are united to Him, then just as by natural kinship you participate in the guilt of the transgressor, so by spiritual kinship you communicate in the grace of the Just One. If you are united to Him in this way, be certain that what belongs to Him will belong to you; what belongs to the Father will belong to the children, and what belongs to the Head will belong to the members: *Wherever the body is, there the eagles will be gathered together* (Mt 24:28).

This is what King David said, in a figure of this mystery, when he spoke to a fearful and confused man, *Join with me, that what will be mine will be yours, and you will be safe with me*[e] (1 Sm 22:23).

Do not look at your weaknesses, which will cause you to faint, but look up to the One who cures, and you will take heart and

---

[e] This is a literal translation of the text employed by St. John of Avila in Spanish, but it does not match any English translation of 1 Sm 22:23 which are like this one from the RSV translation:

Stay with me, fear not; for he that seeks my life seeks your life; with me you shall be in safekeeping.

make an effort. If crossing the river you begin to faint when looking down at the running water, raise your eyes on high and look at the merits of the Crucified, and you will be secure.

If you are tormented by the evil spirit of distrust, sound the harp of David, which is Jesus Christ with the cross. Cast your cares on God (Ps 55:22), and be assured of His providence in the midst of your trials. And if you really believe that the Father gave you His Son, also believe that He will give you everything else, since everything else is less.

16.

Christ is Still Present

Do not think that because He ascended to heaven that you have been forgotten, because you cannot be both loved and forgotten. He left you the greatest pledge that He had when He ascended there, namely the canopy of his precious flesh in memory of His love.

O see that not only when living, did He suffer for you, but even after death He suffered the greatest of His wounds.

And know that in life and death He is your true friend, and understand in this way what He said at the moment He died, *It is finished* (Jn 19:3), that even though His pains ended, His love did not end.

Jesus Christ, says St. Paul, *is the same yesterday and today and for ever* (Heb 13:8). For what He was in this world when He lived for those who loved Him, such is He now and such will He ever be for all who seek Him, love Him and desire Him.

O may you live, my soul, in everlasting gratitude to such a Lord and such a Lover.

Treatise on the Priesthood

1.

The Reason for the Ministerial Priesthood

Being a Priest as a Gift of God

Among all the works that the Divine Majesty accomplishes in the Church through the ministry of men, the priestly office holds the primacy of excellence and obliges the greatest thanksgiving and esteem. Through the priestly ministry, bread and wine are changed into the body and blood of Our Lord Jesus Christ. His divine person is then present through a real presence under the same appearances of bread as were there before the consecration. It is very good to recognize this favor in order to give thanks to the Lord who accomplishes it, and also in order to use it well. As St. Ambrose says, this cannot be done unless the favor is first recognized.[1] But who will have vision keen enough to fix his eyes on the abyss of the splendor of God, from whose heart such a work proceeds? So full of marvels is this work and so revelatory of His ineffable knowledge, immense power, and infinite goodness, that it is called the *glory of God*, to use the expression of the glorious St. Ignatius.[2]

If we try to compare the incomparable sublimity of the priestly office, it will be like comparing a courtier of the king's chamber, who deals with the king's own person, with a peasant who needs the help of this favorite of the king. The peasant kneels before the courtier, kissing his hands and humbly begging his intercession with the king with whom the courtier deals. If we want to compare priests with kings—even though they are monarchs—they exceed them to the same degree as gold exceeds lead, as St. Ambrose puts it.[3]

The Opinion of the People of God

Earthly men, whether of low or high station, whose power is over bodies and bodily things, should not be offended by being surpassed by the priests of God, whose power is over souls. They have the power to open or close heaven to souls and, what is more, they have power over God himself. They bring Him to the altar and to their hands. Even the angels of heaven, including the highest of the seraphim, recognize the advantage of men on earth who are ordained as priests. These angels acknowledge that, even though they are higher in nature and blessed with the vision of God, they do not have power to consecrate God as the poor priest has.

The angels are not envious because they are full of true charity. When in the hands of the priest they see the very Son of God whom they adore and praise in heaven with profound humility and much trembling, they are amazed at the divine goodness that so extends itself. Rejoicing greatly in the happiness of priests, once and many times, with deep desire, they say, *Priests of the Lord, bless the Lord; praise and exalt him above all forever* (Dan 3:84). Seeing priests so honored by God, the angels also honor them and hear with trembling the holy words that come from their mouths. They adore their very King and Lord in the priest's hands, as once and many times they adored Him in the arms of the Virgin Mary. Understanding this, who will not exclaim with the Prophet David, *Who will declare the powers of the Lord? Who will set forth all his praises?*[f] (Ps 106:2).[4] Who will not say, *Come and see the works of God, who is most kind and gracious towards His priests*[g] (Ps 45:9)?[5] Through the ministry of priests, God is not content to convert *the sea into dry*

---

[f] This translation of the Latin (see endnote) can be found in the Douay-Rheims version.

[g] This does not appear in the RSV translation. The Douay-Rheims version reads as follows: *Come and behold ye the works of the Lord: what wonders he hath done upon earth...*

land (Ps 65:6)[h], as He did through the hand of His servant Moses. Rather He converts bread and wine into the body and blood of God himself. Oh, great goodness of God that so exalts priests and raises them up from the dust and the dunghill (cf Ps 112:7)[i]. He gives them power, not only like the princes of His people, but even more, so that they may do what princes cannot do!

Mary and the Priestly Ministry

What more remains when a poor worm of a man can be so lifted up from the earth? The only thing that remains is to compare him with the Blessed Virgin, Mother of the Lord, who is placed higher than angels and men. We shall find that, although in some things the Virgin surpasses priests, in others they are equal to her, and in still others, they surpass her. Who will not be ecstatic at this favor that is beyond the human being's capacity to understand? The Blessed Virgin Mary gave the Word of God His being as man, begetting Him from her most pure blood and becoming His true natural mother. In this no one was, is, or will be her equal. But the sacramental being which the priest gives to God made man, through so exalted a means, is similar to what Mary gave. It is a being that at first the Word did not have. Therefore, the priest is not called the father or mother of God, but a minister of a new being that the Lord previously lacked.

But there is an advantage in which the priest surpasses the Holy Virgin. Only once did she give Him His human being, whereas the priest gives Him His sacramental being every day and as many times as he wants, whenever he does what must be done to consecrate validly. She begot Christ passible, mortal and who came to live in poverty, humility and scorn. Priests consecrate Christ in glory, radiant, immortal and impassible. Having completed the

---

[h] This would be Psalm 66 in the RSV, though it is Psalm 95 in the Douay-Rheims version and the Latin Vulgate.

[i] This can be found in the Douay-Rheims version, although in the RSV, it is Psalm 113.

time of His arduous pilgrimage and His work of serving men, He ascended to heaven and is now reigning over every creature, adored and reverenced by all. Being on a throne of such Majesty, He returns to the hands of the priest through the words of consecration to be enclosed within the small host. Despite the brief space of time in which the Mass is said, it fulfills that honorable word said of the day in which Joshua commanded the sun and the moon not to move and they obeyed. They did it in this way: God obeyed the word of the man, and so it turned out that that day was much longer than all the others were.

The moment of the consecration is brief, if we consider the time it takes. But if we look at the work that God accomplishes through the hands of man, the time is much longer than that other day and even than a thousand other days. There creatures obeyed the word of Joshua (Jos 10:13-14), because God commanded them to obey it. But here, the Lord Himself is the one who comes at the call of the priest. He is present in the consecrated host with such firmness that He will consent to the destruction of heaven and earth rather than be absent from the consecrated host. This is because He holds the truth of His word in higher esteem than the value of creatures. So great a truth is this that if the body of the Lord were not "in the nature of the things," and the words of consecration were said by that very fact, His body and blood would be made again, because the truth of God's words is not lacking. His words accomplish what they signify.

In the Mystery of Christ

These and other considerations were in the mind of St. Gregory when he said: *O venerable dignity of priests in whose hands, as in the womb of the Virgin, the Son of God is incarnate. O sacred and heavenly mystery, which the Father, Son, and Holy Spirit celebrate through us! In one and the same moment, the same God who presides in heaven is in our hands in the Sacrament of the altar. Heaven looks on in wonder; earth gazes with admiration; man reveres; hell looks in horror; the devil begins to tremble; and the angelic height venerates with all its strength.*[6] There are also the words of St. Bernard: *O venerable sanctity of these hands; O happy exercise; O truly the joy of the world! Christ the priest deals with Christ, the Son of God, who delights to be with the children of men. Who has seen anything like this? "He who created me without me, is created through me".*[7] Let us go no farther into such a deep ocean. For it is intolerable to remain silent, and yet impossible to speak in accord with the dignity of this grace. Honoring it more than investigating it, and raising the heart to God, let us say many times, Praised be God; blessed be God! Let many thanks be given to God because He has given such great power to men! Such words are very appropriate for this sacred mystery since it is called a sacrifice of praise, a mystical blessing, and Eucharist, a word that means the action of thanksgiving. For when the Lord instituted this admirable mystery, He blessed and gave thanks to the Father, because He knew that men could not give thanks, or rather could not give the thanks that were suitable. Therefore, knowing the value of the grace, He gave thanks. He exercised His pontifical office, to which it pertains to intercede with the Father for us for what we need, and to give thanks to the Father for what comes to us through His prayer. *To Him be glory forever. Amen.* (Rv 1:6).[8]

The Dignity of Serving

Those who look superficially at high offices without a deeper consideration of the obligations they involve, are deceived and, more than that, they are greatly harmed. Dazzled by the exterior splendor which attracts the eye, they throw themselves without reflection into what appears from the outside to be so greatly honored, delightful and certain. But afterwards, it turns out to be very dangerous for them and a cause of grave condemnation, because they have accepted an obligation for which they have neither merit nor strength. The sweeter it was for them to accept the office, the more bitter is the cost. Although too late, they come to understand how much greater care and presence it takes for one who walks on the heights to avoid falling. They also understand how much more serious it is to fall from a height than to fall while walking on level ground. It would be good for anyone who receives a high office to consider the strict accounting to be rendered. Because, the higher the station of the wife, the greater the responsibility of the husband in fulfilling his obligations to her.

Priestly Sanctity: Living What We Are

The priestly office is very high, as has been said. St. Ambrose expresses this: *Nothing in this world is more excellent than the priesthood.* But as he also says: *What we are by profession, let us demonstrate in action rather than by name. Let the name be appropriate to the action, and let the action correspond with the name. Do not let the name be an empty word and an immense crime; do not let it be a sublime honor and a deformed way of life. Do not let it be a deifying profession and an illicit action; do not let it be a religious covering and an irreligious fruit. Do not let it be the highest grade and ugly excess; do not let the seat be very sublime and the conscience of the priest be found to be base.*[9] Finally, high office is a monstrous thing in the unworthy; also monstrous are a high station and a low life, as St. Bernard says, *A monstrous thing is the highest degree when the spirit is the lowest, the highest place and the lowest way of life.*[10]

If the priest wants to know the wealth of virtue necessary for fulfilling well the obligations of such a high and holy office, let him hear the Holy Church in the Offertory of the Mass of the Blessed Sacrament: *The priests of the Lord offer incense and bread to God; therefore they shall be holy to their God.*[11] The Church took these words from what the Lord said to the priests of the Old Law, *You shall be holy because I, the Lord your God, am holy* (Prv 21:14)[j]. If we hear these words with the faith and reverence due to them and

---

[j] This is not a correct citation. A similar quote may be found, as referring to priests, in Lev. 21:8.

consider our great weakness, they will cause us great confusion. For we see what great sanctity is asked of us, and it may be that we do not even possess average goodness. Oh, how quickly we pass over this business and how little we feel the obligation it demands of us! How little fear we have of placing ourselves into such an office and how little care for carrying it out well once we have it! May it please God that at some point we feel compunction and supply with tears for what we lack of the required sanctity.

Some may think that too much holiness is asked of priests. But if they hear the reason for it, perhaps they will see that even if such sanctity were not demanded, it could justly be demanded.

Facing God and Men: Prayer and Sacrifice

Do you ask, Mother Church, that we, your priests, be holy? Why impose a burden so great that even hearing about it makes one tremble?

She declares the answer, saying, *The priests offer incense and bread to God.* Is it such a great thing to incense the altar and place the loaves of proposition upon the table of the temple? O God, give me strength! Who would think that God would require holiness in His ministers to do something for which an average purity seems enough? But it is as with other things of Old Testament times. Externally they appeared to be of little importance, but, within themselves, they were carrying very precious mysteries. So the incense and bread were pointing to the priestly ministry of the New Law. This ministry consists in offering to the Lord the incense of pleasing and efficacious prayer to calm His anger, and in consecrating and offering the bread that came down from heaven, Our Lord Jesus Christ. As far as the heavens are above the earth, and much more than that, He exceeds the bread and sacrifice of the Old Law.

O God, give me strength! What a great business are holy prayer and consecration and offering the body of Jesus Christ! The holy Church joins them together because for actions and beings of such worth to be done well, they have to go together.

It is fitting for the priest to pray because he is a mediator between God and men. So that his prayer may not be without fruit, he offers the gift that calms God's anger, Jesus Christ, our Lord. To him apply the words, *a hidden gift extinguishes wrath*.[12] The priest has the obligation to pray, not in any way he wants, but with great quiet and a fragrance delightful to God, as physical incense is to men. Since this obligation is so neglected, and even unknown, as though it did not exist, it will be helpful to speak about it at some length. If we do this with light drawn from the Word of God and the sayings of His saints, our blindness will be enlightened and, recognizing our obligation, we will then be moved to ask the Lord for strength to accomplish it.

2.

Prayer as a Priestly Task

Responsibility for All Humanity

Saint John Chrysostom said: *For the one who is intercessor on behalf of the city . . ., what am I saying, "on behalf of the city"? Rather he carries out his mission for the whole world and implores the mercy of God against all evils, not only those of the living but also of the dead, as you think necessary. I do not think that even confidence in Moses and Elijah suffices. For indeed the whole universe is committed to him, praying that any fighting anywhere be extinguished and that he be father to all. Thus he approaches God, begging that any battles anywhere be extinguished and disturbances calmed and that an end come to all evils, private and public. Thus, an intercessor has to differ in eminence of virtue from that of all men, so that he excels all, and by the same distance as his office is different.* Thus spoke Chrysostom.[13]

These are frightening words. They oblige the priest to pray for the whole world to obtain goods and placate evils. So great is the office with its obligation to pray that even the confidence of Moses and Elijah is too small to carry it out. By the force of his prayer, Moses won pardon for his numerous army. When it seemed good to him, Elijah closed up the heavens so that it did not rain and opened them so that it did. He brought fire from on high that killed the living, and with the same prayer, he gave life to the dead. He also miraculously brought fire to burn the sacrifices, as a testimony that the Lord is the true God.

Prayer of Mediation

The divine Scripture tells that, when the fire of just punishment coming from God was burning the camp in the desert, the priest Aaron took the censor in his hand. Standing between the living and the dead, he calmed God's anger by incensing and praying. Woe to us that we do not have the gift of prayer with which to hold back God's hands from vengeance when He says, "Leave me so that I may exercise my wrath. Nor do we have such sanctity of life that we can conquer the Unconquerable One. I do not know if we even understand the word "prayer" since, as St. Augustine says, this business is better done with sighs than with words. The only one who can sigh as is necessary for his prayer to have this efficacious power, is the one to whom the Holy Spirit, through His holiness and goodness alone, has taught such prayer.

St. Paul is witness to this in these words: *Likewise the Spirit also helps our infirmity. For we know not what we should pray for as we ought, but the Spirit Himself asks for us with unspeakable groanings* (Rm 8:26). Man's vision is very weak for knowing what should be asked and how to ask for it. Many times he asks for what is not fulfilled and even for what would injure him, as is seen with the sons of Zebedee and also with St. Paul. If this is true for them, how much more so for us? But it is this weakness and ignorance in something so important that the Holy Spirit remedies by teaching us to pray *according to God*, as St. Paul says with authority (Rm 8:27). He means that the Spirit teaches us to ask for what God wants us to ask, and for what He wants to give by means of our prayer. For it is a true statement that what God before the ages ordained to give in time, He wanted to be effected through the prayer of his own. It is about this prayer that we are speaking. It always achieves what it asks because it is inspired by the Holy Spirit, whose works do not come forth in vain.

Thus, says St. Ambrose, asking the aid of the prayers of others, *You never spurn the prayers of such men, Lord, if You Yourself have inspired them to pray for me.*[14] Such was the prayer of Moses when he obtained pardon for the people, and such was the prayer of many others (cf. Ex 32:30-32). The prayer of the priest should be the same for God has placed him in the same office. Consequently, he should be excellent in his office and in its works, and not just equal to those who do not hold the office, but surpassing them. Thus, when the Lord wants to do some good through the prayer of the priest, He inspires him to ask. The priest then asks for what God inspires with such affection and confidence that it leaves traces in his soul, and he thinks that his prayer has been efficacious. At times the Lord inspires prayers for general intentions such as the conversion of unbelievers or the good of the Church. At other times, He inspires prayers for particular persons. Not infrequently, when the priest wants to pray for one person, another comes to his mind and goes ahead of the first person. The priest is then moved to pray with great affection for the second person even though he was not remembering him nor thinking about praying for him. In the end, he does not pray for the person he wanted to pray for at first, or at least, he prays less for him.

In Divine Intimacy

This communication of the Lord with the priest, through the Holy Spirit in which He announces his will concerning the good things He desires to do or the punishments He intends to send. is a deal among friends. These latter He makes known in order to receive prayers to remove His scourges and to bestow graces through the priest. It is as the Lord says, *I have called you friends, because all things that I have heard from My Father, I have made known to you* (Jn 15:15). Just as the Old Testament priest has to inquire of the Law of the Lord, because he is its messenger, as Malachi says (2:7) so too does the New Testament priest have to inquire what is the will of God in this or that. Because he is a person who has a special friendship and personal association with God, we believe that the Lord will not refrain from telling the priest whatever he wants to know for the good of his neighbors.

It appears in the Old Testament that the priest of the Lord was often consulted to know God's will, for example, whether to go to war or not, and other similar things. Even the pagans of the past followed the same custom, as even now do those who are found in the Indies. Both groups ask their false priests what they have to do in particular matters so that these latter may bring them a response from their false gods. Receiving these, they go off quite content. This shows how common among men is the sense that priests have special friendship and dealings with God, that He hears their prayers, and that He does good to men through them. Thus, they are not only called helpers of God, as St. Paul says (1 Cor 3:9), because through the exercise of their holy word and administration of the holy sacraments, they help God to save souls. But they are also helpers, and very great ones, in that through their prayer, they ensure that their preaching and good works are done with fruit. Also, through prayer alone, they ensure that they achieve good things and avoid evil. This prayer is not lukewarm. As St. Bernard says, *Any prayer which is not preceded by inspiration is tepid.*[15] The Lord says, *If you offer blind animals for sacrifice, is it not evil?* (Mal 1:8). According to St. Jerome, this means that the prayer the priest offers to the Lord must not be blind with regard to what he asks and must not be governed by a human spirit, but must be made with the light of the Holy Spirit. Neither should it be poor or weak but efficacious, attentive, and very strong.[16] This is what St. Paul means when he says, *the Spirit himself asks for us with unspeakable groanings* (Rm 8:26). It is not because the Holy Spirit groans or prays within Himself, for He is God and cannot suffer. Neither is the one who asks, superior to the Holy Spirit. Rather it is because, through His inspiration, He makes us ask for what He wants us to ask, and for what He wants to give. We do not do this lukewarmly, but with very deep groans caused by the Holy Spirit. Those who have no experience of these groans cannot possibly understand them, and even those who do have them, cannot recount them. Because He acts so powerfully to make us ask, it is said that He is the one who asks.

The Priestly Sentiments of Christ

The priest at the altar in the Mass represents Our Lord Jesus Christ, the principal priest and source of our priesthood. It is very right that anyone who imitates Him in his office, should imitate Him also in the groans, prayer, and tears that He poured out for the sins of the world in the Mass that he celebrated on the cross on Good Friday. *And He was heard for His reverence* (Heb 5:7),[17] as St. Paul says. The priest has to see himself in this priestly mirror in order to be conformed to Him in his desires and prayer. Offering Christ before the majesty of the Father for the sins and healing of the world, the priest must also offer himself—his possessions, his honor, his very life—for himself and for the whole world. In this way, he will be heard, according to his measure and his likeness to Christ in prayer and groans.

The words of St. Gregory confirm what has been said. *It is necessary that when we do these things, we offer ourselves to God with a contrite heart, for when we celebrate the mysteries of the Lord, we must imitate what we are doing.*[18] This shows how necessary for us is the gift of the Holy Spirit who teaches us to pray. For only the one who has the Spirit of Jesus Christ is able to pray as He did. St. Ambrose understood this very well when he prayed with great intensity for the grace of the Holy Spirit so that he might worthily celebrate these divine mysteries.[19]

Fervent devotion is the tongue with which the soul speaks with God in this kind of prayer that St. Bernard speaks about.[20] Since this tongue is of heaven and moved by a heavenly spirit, it knows very well how to plead in the tribunal of divine mercy for its intentions and for the intentions of those entrusted to it. For what comes from heaven, ascends to heaven, while one who is of the earth, speaks of the earth and remains on the earth.

St. Ambrose said[21] that tears and prayer are the weapons of priests. Armed with these, even though they are very gentle, the priest struggles with great confidence against the justice of God, offering himself as another Moses to be a wall against which God could discharge His wrath, and pour out His mercy on the people (cf Ex 32:9-14, 31-32). The people, with their evil way of life, are frightened and do not have the audacity to stand before the majesty of God or even to raise their eyes to heaven. The Lord wills that the priest be such that, because of his purity of life and the friendship and particular familiarity that exist between God and him, he should not be overcome with fear as the people are. Rather, he should possess a holy audacity to stand before the Lord and to approach Him, to implore Him and to pester Him, to bind Him and to conquer Him, so that instead of the heavy blows of a just Judge, He may send the embraces of a loving Father.

Sensitivity to the Interests of God and the Problems of Men

We can see this in the fact that in the holy sacrifice of the Mass, the people kneel humbly, striking their breasts, full of fear and confusion because of their sins. The priest, on the other hand, is standing at the altar, dealing with God about the remedy for the sins of the people. He carries to them the olive branch, the symbol of peace, just as the dove carried it to those on Noah's ark who were frightened by the scourge of the great flood. The priest triumphs over God Himself who, in His great mercy, decided to give such power and ministry to men, so that they might struggle with Him and conquer Him, using the tender arms of tears and prayer. The priest, as Origen says, is the face of the Church.[22] Just as the beauty of the whole body shines forth in the face, so the clergy must be the outstanding beauty of the whole Church. The eyes are placed in the face not only to give light to the whole body so that it does not stumble, but also to weep for its falls and for all the other evils that come to it in any way. It is as though the eyes themselves were wounded. So too the priest must have two eyes like the two pools in Heshbon (Sng 7:4) with which he may weep for offenses against God and for the perdition of souls. He must transform within himself the labors and sins of others and feel them as his own, so that he can represent them before the majesty of God's mercy with compassionate affection and a paternal heart. The priest must have such a heart towards all, like the Lord, and also like St. Ambrose, who said that he did not love his spiritual children any less than he would have if he had begotten them in marriage.[23] St. John Chrysostom says that priests must love their spiritual children even more than they would have loved natural children.[24] Priests must be warned that it is not right to have, in vain or as a lie, the name of "father" which we give them. Rather, they must have within themselves paternal and maternal affection so that they may be helpful to their neighbors and pray and weep for them.

If every Christian must plead with compassion and weep for those who weep, with how much greater reason must it be done by one who has the responsibility by his office? For the priest is supposed to beg alms for the poor, health for the sick, ransom for the imprisoned, pardon for the guilty, life for the dead, preservation of life for the living, and conversion for unbelievers. In short, should not the priest seek, through prayer and sacrifice, to apply to men the great good that the Savior won for them on the Cross? If any among the priests wept for the dead son as another widow of Naim (Lk 7:11ff), pestered the Lord as the Canaanite woman did (Mt 15:22ff), offered devout prayers for the possessed son who sometimes threw himself into fire and other times into water (Mt 17:14ff), the Lord would always console them saying, *Do not weep* (Lk 7:13). He would always give them souls risen and healthy just as he gave bodily health and life to other people. Perhaps He would also give spiritual health for their children.

Lack of Priestly Prayer

Because there is a lack of such prayer in the Church, and especially in the priesthood, which St. Gregory[25] calls the principal part of the Church, the Lord has poured out His wrath upon us and will not remove it until this prayer returns. Its absence has been the cause of many hardships, and may it please God that greater ones may not come. The prophet Isaiah saw in spirit the captivity of the kingdom of Judah and understood that lack of prayer was its cause. Speaking with God of his sorrow, he said, *There is no one who invokes Your name, no one who rises up and takes hold of You* (Is 59:4)[k]. St. Jerome saw in his time the terrible scourge of war that God sent upon Rome and complained that there was no one in his time that opposed the wrath of the Lord in order to prevent His severe punishment.[26] As the Church has the same lack of prayer now, it is impossible to excuse the sorrow of the present or the fear of the future.

---

[k] Both the Douay-Rheims and the RSV versions differ from the quote as cited here. The RSV version reads as follows: *No one enters suit justly, no one goes to law honestly; they rely on empty pleas, they speak lies, they conceive mischief and bring forth iniquity.*

From what has already been said, it is clear how rightly God and His holy Church demand sanctity in priests. To them has been entrusted the high office of being intercessors between God and his Church. In order to be this properly, a very great gift of prayer is required. May it be as efficacious as the Holy Spirit asks. For this, as St. Gregory says,[27] the one begging must be a friend of the one from whom he begs.

3.

Sacrifice: Being a Victim with Christ the Priest

Mediating Sacrifice

It remains to clarify the other reason for which sanctity is demanded, the other reason why it is good, that is, *because they offer bread to God* (cf. Lev 21:6). If this holiness was asked of those who would place some loaves of bread made from wheat on the table, how much greater reason is there for demanding holiness of those who offer the bread that came down from heaven to give life to the world and also to heaven! Holiness means purity. If sanctity is not required to touch the most pure body of Christ our Lord, the holiest thing of all, I do not know for what it is needed on earth. If St. Paul says that the woman who is a virgin must be "holy in body and spirit", how much greater reason is there for the one who holds a more excellent office to be holy! Paul asks the same sanctity of body and spirit of those in Corinth so that they may participate in the promises of God. How much more must he be holy in body and spirit who not only awaits promises, but has received the priestly ministry from the compassionate hand of God, a great grace, as St. Ambrose considers it.

Since we have little esteem for the infinite Majesty of God and little of the respect due to His divine worship, it will probably seem that to demand such sanctity in His ministers is somewhat excessive and offensive. But since the Divine Majesty knows Himself, He very justly asks for such sanctity and purity in those who approach His altar. That this was so even in the time when irrational animals were offered to Him is a cause of wonder in those who consider the matter. Who would think that a priest would be considered unclean for touching a corpse, or carrying it to burial, or accompanying the funeral party? The same was true if he touched a dead chicken or carried the ashes of the animal commanded by the Lord for the expiation of sins. Who would think that for any of these things, or for others which appear even more trivial, the priest became unclean and was unable to approach the altar without cleansing himself of that uncleanness by the remedies which God had ordained? But the Most High God, whose works are truth and justice, considered those who had fallen into these things as unclean and therefore unable to deal with His sacrifices. He was not looking so much at the things themselves as at what was signified by them. Through that visible and corporal purity, He wanted it understood what great sanctity, separate from all defilement, is necessary for handling things pertaining to divine worship. Let us consider how far surpassing all else it is that God comes at the call of the priest, that He is present in his hands, and that He allows the priest to treat Him with a familiarity so intimate that no one would have thought it possible. No sanctity will seem excessive or equal, or even sufficient compared to that which the Lord of infinite purity deserves as He shares Himself in such an ineffable communion.

Intimacy with Christ

God is truth and all His works are true. He bestowed such holiness upon His sacrifices that what they signify from the outside, they accomplish from within. Whoever receives the sacrifices of

God must have the same intent and correspondence between the exterior and the interior. If a person occupies himself only with the exterior aspects of the sacrifice, he does not receive its fruit. On the contrary, it harms him because of the lack of respect he has for such a holy thing. It is unbelievable that God, who is such a friend of truth in all His works and sacrifices, would not want to be the same in the familiar relationships of His most holy body. For these relationships are so friendly that there is nothing like them on earth. For the truth to be maintained, there has to be a love of Christ for the priest and of the priest for Christ. There must be an intimate interior friendship between the two and a resemblance in their way of life. They must love and abhor in the same manner. In short, the love between them must be so deep that the two become one and the words of the Lord are fulfilled: *He that eats My flesh, and drinks My blood, abides in Me, and I in him* (Jn 6:57). So too are fulfilled the words of St. Paul: *Whoever is joined with God is one spirit with Him* (1 Cor 6:17). Let no one be deceived. The aptitude for the office has to be in conformity with the office. An office requiring so much love and familiarity does not befit everyone, but only those who have a particularly intimate familiarity, friendship, and conversation with God within their souls.

The office itself is a witness to this truth. So too are the names given to the priest. He is called "angel" because as far as possible he should have angelic purity. He is the "temple" of God, and for that reason, has to be holy, as St. Paul says (1 Cor 3:17). Sacred Scripture calls priests "gods" because they have to be more than human(cf. Ps 81:6[1]). As St. Dionysius says, *Whoever has said priesthood means all the Holy Orders at once; thus whoever says "priest," even more strictly implies a godlike man.*[28] Whoever is going to deal with divinity must be divine. He must be especially converted to that Lord, whom so many times he consecrates and receives sacramentally. When the holy prophet, Moses, dealt with the di-

---

[1] This would be Psalm 82 in the RSV, though it is Psalm 81 in the Douay-Rheims version and the Latin Vulgate.

vine Majesty for a short time, he became so full of light and so superhuman that no one could look at him unless he covered the splendor of his face. How much greater reason there is to demand that the priest be light for the world and cause admiration in those who look at him! When he is so exalted in the knowledge and experience of divine things, how much more necessary it is that he descend so that men in their weaknesses might benefit from him.

Sign of Christ the Victim

St. Jerome says[29] that the maiden dedicated to God is a sacrifice belonging to God and that it is necessary to take advantage of this for the sacrifice sanctifies what it touches. For this reason, speaking with her, , hearing her or seeing her should be a cause of sanctification for those who deal with her. With how much greater reason is this said of the priest! If he is what he should be, not only does he have to be a sacrifice, but a holocaust, entirely offered to God and burnt by the fire of divine love in honor of God. That Lord, who is the source of light, and who so often comes to the priest's house, fills him with such holiness that its rays come forth from the priest through his eyes, his mouth, his behavior and his uprightness. Everything about the priest declares that he is the ark of God's covenant and a reliquary of God. So filled is he with delight in God that all who hear him, speak with him, or see him, however lacking in devotion and distracted they may be, nonetheless sense the divine power which is within the priest. As St. Gregory says,[30] this is what it means to be the salt of the earth when that expression is truly understood. If the priest should want to forget all this, he should look at himself from head to toe when he is clothed in the holy vestments. If he does not think of the vestments merely from outside, he will understand the virtue which each of them signifies. These are neither of little account nor are they few in number. The priest should make the effort to have these virtues in his soul, so as to avoid the deception of having the clothing outside while lacking within what they signify. In such a case, those who go to seek Christ in the priest will find nothing there to take except the linen cloth and the napkin in which he was wrapped for burial (Jn 20:5-7).

The Physiognomy of Christ

Whoever reflects carefully on the soul and body of a good priest who has the virtues demanded by his high office will not be mistaken in comparing him with an earthly paradise, planted with a diversity of trees which are not less beautiful than fruitful. The tree of life which is Jesus Christ our Lord is planted in the middle of this paradise . He is received by the priest and placed in his heart to give him life, a life that never ends. This is the garden which is ever more abundant than that of King Ahasuerus or King Solomon, whose gardens, planted by human hands and watered by earthly water, gave earthly fruit that lasted only a moment. Here, the Holy Spirit is the one who plants the virtues and waters them with His grace through the merits of Jesus Christ. The fruit taken from this garden is a pure fruit: peace beyond all understanding and many other excellent fruits for the priest himself and for the whole Church. These fruits are picked now. Afterwards there is eternal life.

The High Priest of the Old Law had many precious stones on his vestments when he entered to sacrifice to the Lord. But that office was a mere shadow and almost nothing in comparison with the priestly office of the New Law, by which the very Son of God is consecrated and received. Reason then requires that, instead of earthly stones brought forth from the earth, our priests should be adorned with precious virtues come from heaven, infused by God. Since there are so many of these, and we would never finish counting them one by one, we can leave their numbering to the one who counts the multitude of the stars of heaven, and to what the saints say. We will speak briefly and very little about this extensive subject.

Priestly Chastity

We are asked to be pure in body and soul, as has been said above, in order to consecrate the Lord and to receive Him with profit. We begin with bodily purity. It is clear then how just and right it is that the most pure body of Jesus Christ should be received and dealt with through the hands of a priest who is absolutely pure. Among the modes of purity required of the priest, that of chastity is neither the least necessary nor the least pleasing to the Lord. This virtue, which is proper, very proper, and most proper for the priest of the gospel, is seen figuratively in the priesthood of the Old Law. God commanded the Old Testament priest that in the time when he had to offer sacrifices to Him, he should separate himself from relations with his wife. Among the vestments which He demanded that he should wear were *linen breeches to cover their shame* (cf Ex 28:42).[31] If he did not wear them, he was to die (cf Ex 28:42-43). This shows us that, since in the priesthood, we are always about to offer sacrifice—a most pure sacrifice which loves and creates all purity—we have to be clothed with the virtue of chastity. We must have our flesh bound by the rules of discipline, if we wish to avoid the eternal death that is threatened to the impure that offer this sacrifice to God.

God loves this purity very much, and He has given very great signs that His holy will is that His sacred body be handled by hands and bodies that are pure. In testimony of this, when He took on our flesh, He also took on our weaknesses, and thus He suffered hunger, thirst, weariness, and death itself. All this He did to our great advantage since He took on more of all this than we ourselves take. But in the matter of being conceived through the pleasure of conjugal relations between a man and a woman, He was not like us. Rather He desired to be conceived in the very purest way, different and far removed from all immodesty. He was conceived through the work of the Virgin Mother and through the work of the Holy Spirit. This shows that a body so pure in spirit must be handled and received by a body that is likewise spiritual, as far as possible. When the one is in complete harmony with the other, due proportion is preserved, and there is joy on the part of each because each one loves the other and rejoices with it. . We can understand this from the fact that, as a child, the Lord desired to be touched by the hands of a Virgin and to rest in her arms and on her breast. At the time of His death, He was wrapped in a sheet of pure, white linen and placed in a tomb that had not received anyone before Him. This was the understanding of the Supreme Pontiffs of the past, enlightened by the Spirit of the Lord, who shows men what pleases God. They commanded that anyone who wants to be a priest, must be a virgin, or at least, that he should be married only once, and then, to a virgin.

In the Old Law

No one should wonder at this purity that the Son of God asks of those who must deal intimately with Him and be joined with Him. In the Old Law, the High Priest was commanded not to marry anyone except a woman of certain qualities, the principal one being that she should be a virgin. Who does not see how right it is for a girl, set aside to be the spouse of a powerful king, to be brought up completely apart from any impurity? Should she not be taught how unworthy it would be to marry the great king if her virginity were not very complete and pure? If such purity is demanded to receive the priestly office, as is right, is it not much more proper that after the office has been received, the priest should not soil his body with the mire of carnal delight? This would be a grave offense against the author of purity who deigned to join the priest with Himself, and thus obliged him anew not to give his body to anyone to whom it did not belong.

Apostolic Inheritance

The holy apostles, illuminated by the Holy Spirit, realized very well the gravity of this offense when they commanded that the priest who fell into fornication, by that very fact, would never again in his life, consecrate or handle the holy body of Christ. Rather, since he had been placed in honor—and in such honor—and did not recognize it, he was to lose the exercise of the office for which he was so ungrateful. Afterwards, some Pontiffs, moved with compassion for human weakness, decided to moderate this just rigor with mercy. But even with all that, through a great and very particular grace, they extended the penance imposed to ten years—a somewhat harsh penance—for the one that had fallen into this sin. When the penance had been well completed, and the guilty priest had given hope of repentance and true amendment, he returned to the exercise of the office he had lost.

No one should think that this penalty is excessively severe. If it does appear that way to anyone, he should understand that he does not possess the Spirit of the Lord. Christ himself said of him that does, *He will glorify me; because He will receive of Mine* (Jn 16:14).[32] In another place, He said, *He will give testimony of Me* (Jn 15:26).[33] It is the work of the Holy Spirit to magnify Christ in the hearts where He dwells. Just as He pronounces Christ worthy of all honor and glory, so He pronounces every sin against Him evil and worthy of grave torments. Whoever, in the light of the Holy Spirit, considers the "terrible hour" (which is the way the saints describe it) when the priest is at the altar and consecrates the Son of God, will see clearly what great purity and noble qualities are demanded to carry it out well. The priest has to have kept himself throughout his life from anything impure. Thus, he may go to the altar as composed in spirit as the pure virgin enters the wedding chamber of her spouse, adorned in rich clothes and fragrant with perfume, lacking nothing that her spouse could desire in her.

The Thought of the Fathers

Since we are so far from thinking in this way and the question is important for our life, it will be well for us to hear and follow the saints. Enlightened by the Holy Spirit, they judged all things as spiritual men, including the question of the reverence and holiness needed in that hour to touch the Sacred Body of Christ Our Lord in a way pleasing to Him.

Let us begin with the Blessed Saint Chrysostom[34] who says, "Therefore a suppliant must differ from everyone in eminence of virtue in the same measure as he excels and differs from them in his office; and when he shall call upon the Holy Spirit, and immolate that host to be reverenced, where, tell me, shall we put him in our estimation? How much splendor and how much religion shall demand from him? Consider now how his hands ought to be, that are the ministers of such great things, what tongue ought to be pouring out Christ, or with what fire his soul ought to be cleaner or holier?..."

"Then also even the Angels surround the priest, and the Tribunal and the place of the altar is filled with heavenly Virtues, in honor of the One Who is immolated, which is certainly clear from these things that are considered. I heard, from someone telling it, that a certain priest, admirable for his sanctity of life and who was accustomed to seeing revelations, had maintained that he sometimes saw such a vision at the time of the holy sacrifice, and watched a multitude of angels (as it was possible to look at) with flashing stoles, and an altar crowned with service by which soldiers are accustomed to standing around their king. I was certainly easily persuaded by this."

"Another referred to me that he had heard from another that those withdrawing from this world, who participate in those mysteries in clean continence, when they draw their last breath, are thrown up quickly into the hands of the Angels. Therefore, do you not tremble that you lean on leading me to such a ministry, clothed in filth and vice; and inserting me into the dignity of the priests, me such a one as Christ would have separated from the gathering of those feasting? Thus the priestly soul must shine with splendor of life illuminating the whole world; while ours works evil with much darkness and is bent so that it sometimes dares not to look at his God with trust. Priests are the salt of the earth; who is able to sustain easily our folly and our ignorance in all things, except you, who have decided to love us beyond measure?"

Who does not experience admiration and fear at the words of this Saint who, enlightened by God, knows the excellence and grandeur of this sacrifice and the resplendent purity that the priest's hands must have? For this reason, he considered himself so unworthy that he complained of St. Basil because he had invited him to assume this office.

So that this truth may appear more clearly and that we might be more ashamed of our negligence, let St. Augustine[35] speak: "If even the Angels who adore and praise You tremble, filled with amazing exultation, then I, a sinner, why do I not tremble with fear in my heart, become pallid of countenance, tremble with my lips, and shudder with my whole body while I am present before You and say praises and offer sacrifice? Thus with tears springing up before You I unceasingly deplore. . .I ardently admire, while I see You, too Terrible to the eyes of faith. O miserable me, when I have a heart so hardened! and when my eyes unceasingly do not produce rivers of tears, while a servant converses before His God, a man with God, and a creature with the Creator; he who was made from mud with He Who made all things out of nothing." And after he says: "God, Giver of all good things, give me the font of tears among your praises, together with the purity of heart and jubilation of mind, so that perfectly loving, and praising You worthily, I may feel with the palate of the heart, taste, and understand how sweet and gentle you are, Lord."

His first worry was that, because he did not have this contrition of heart, font of tears, reverence and fear, he was a wicked, and a very wicked servant. What will happen to us who, not having these things, are unashamed and neither ask for them with tears nor fear the judgment of God?

Let the blessed St. Ambrose[36] tell what he experienced when he wanted to celebrate: "Teach me, Your unworthy servant, who among all the rest of your gifts you deigned to call to the priestly office, not by my own merits, but only by the esteem of Your mercy: teach me, I beg, through the Spirit, to treat such mystery with reverence and honor, and with the vocation and fear which are fitting: make me, Lord Jesus Christ, by your grace, always to believe and understand, feel and firmly retain, say and think about such a mystery that which pleases You and is useful to my soul."

And afterwards he says, "Lord Jesus Christ, with how much contrition of heart and fount of tears, with how much reverence and trembling, with how much chastity of body and purity of soul, must that Divine and Heavenly Sacrifice be celebrated, where Your Flesh is truly eaten, where Your Blood is truly drunk."

"Who shall be worthy. ...unless You Yourself shall have made him so? I know, and truly I know, and I confess to Your Truth Itself, that I am not worthy to approach Your ministry on account of my excessive sins and infinite negligences".

St. Jerome[37] says, "Do such therefore, and live in a monastery, so that you may merit to be a cleric, and do not defile your adolescence with anything sordid, so that you may proceed to the altar of Christ as a virgin to her bridal chamber". In these words, he summarizes the purity, spiritual beauty, and adornment of grace that he must take to the altar, things won and worked for throughout his life, as we said in other places. From this can be deduced the sanctity of his life and of his spirit, and with what great care he would celebrate these sacred mysteries. With all his preparation, considering the greatness of this mystery, he did not dare to celebrate it every day.

The great reverence and trembling of St. Gregory[38] when he celebrated has already been mentioned. He says that the priest must celebrate with much contrition of heart and must imitate what he represents.

The Testimony of the Saints

We would lack time and space rather than testimonies and works of saints, who teach us the excellence of holiness that the one who celebrates the sacred mysteries must have. We ought not hear this with deaf ears or put it out of our sight. Rather, we should place these words and examples of holy men right before our eyes. Through them, we recognize our faults, weep over them, and seek remedies for them. This is not my invention. Rather, it is the doctrine that the Lord gave, though figuratively, to the priests of the Old Law. He commanded them that, before they go up to the altar, they should place a great mirror, made of the mirrors of the women who kept watch in the temple (Ex 38:8; cf. Ex 30:17-18). In this mirror, they should look at themselves to see if they were fittingly vested, as God commanded them, to offer the sacrifice acceptable in His eyes. This collection of good examples and words of the saints is the great mirror, made of individual mirrors, each one of which is a testimony in itself. It should not seem unreasonable that these holy men were represented by the weaker sex because women often share in devotion and recollection, and even surpass many men in them. When the divine word says that the mirrors have to be from women who celebrate vigils in the temple, it speaks figuratively of the souls of holy men. Deeply devoted to divine worship, they kept watch in prayer by night, so that by day, they might be well-prepared to celebrate the divine mysteries. They heard clearly the words of the Gospel and took it as addressed to themselves at midnight, *Behold the bridegroom is coming, go forth to meet Him* (Mt 25:6).[39] They considered the burning love with which Christ, the Spouse of souls, would come when it was day, to embrace them, to console them, and to give them graces. Therefore, they exchanged sleep for keeping watch, so that they would be ready to go out to receive with heavenly adornment the heavenly Spouse who was coming within them.

Like the Baptist and St. Peter

In such mirrors, the priest who is going to consecrate, should look at himself. Among these, he should not forget one of the most important, St. John the Baptist. He considered himself unworthy of simply pouring water on Christ's head and said with profound trembling and reverence, *I should be baptized by You and are You coming to me?* (Mt 3:14).[40] On this account, a priest needs greater sanctity and greater fear and wonder since he deals with the Lord more familiarly than did St. John the Baptist.

What shall we say of our blessed father, St. Peter? Considering himself unworthy to be in a boat because Our Lord was there, he cried out, *Depart from me, for I am a sinful man, O Lord* (Lk 5:8).[41] The Lord manifested this profound reverence and religious fear long before through the prophet Malachi, saying, *"My covenant was with him [Levi] of life and peace, and I gave him fear, and he feared Me, and he was afraid before My name* (Mal 2:5).[42] This is the blessed St. Peter, whom the Lord constituted a priest, and a High Priest, a minister of life and of peace, who feared the Lord and trembled in the presence of his name. This means that with the trembling of his body, he was declaring the interior trembling of his soul. This was not the trembling of a slave, for he deeply loved Christ Our Lord. But it was a most profound reverence, proceeding from his awareness of the high dignity of the Lord and of his own lowliness. If he trembled out of reverence merely from being near Our Lord, what would he do when he held Him present and touched Him with his own hands? I think that he would dissolve completely into devout tears of tenderness and reverential love. For we read of him that he could not remember the loving conversation that Our Lord Jesus Christ had with him and the other apostles while living this mortal life, without surrendering his heart to Him and without his eyes becoming fountains of tears. Now, the conversation of the Lord with the priest at the altar is much more familiar, and Peter had greater light and love than he had before the Holy Spirit in His fullness had come upon him. So great would be his feeling, thanksgiving, love, and trembling, that he gave glory to Our Lord and received great consolation for his spirit. But for us, his sons, there is much embarrassment at seeing ourselves so far from the imitation of such a father.

Imitation of the Virgin Mary

Our obligation does not stop here. For, according to what we have said, preparation for the use of an office has to be in conformity with the greatness of its dignity.

We said that priests compete in dignity of life with the Most Holy Virgin Mary, our Patroness, in consecrating and touching the very Son of God. She touched Him when He was a child and in a mortal body; we touch Him now that He is great and glorious as He is in heaven. Such men justly have to make every effort to rival her holiness, if not by equality, at least by resemblance. Oh, how moved to tenderness is the heart of a good priest when, holding the Son of God in his hands, he considers how unworthy those hands are in comparison with those of Our Lady! Certainly, no incentive could be found to so spur him on and make him run the way of perfection as to place in his hands the same Lord of heaven and earth, who was placed in the hands of a Virgin on whom God looked with pleasure, endowing her and making her beautiful with countless virtues. Yet with all this, none of them was too much, considering the dignity of the familiar dealings that she had with the Son of God.

Spirit of Sacrifice

No one should marvel that the grace of prayer, the purity of chastity, and a very special abstinence are demanded of the priest. The last of these was prefigured in God's command to priests of the Old Law (Lev 10:9). At the time the priest is administering his office, he should not drink wine or anything that might intoxicate him. For the body of the Son of God which we are touching is a glorious body, which has a bodily substance, but does not have bodily weaknesses. Since the body of the priest that receives the Lord and handles Him cannot be glorious in this life, let it at least be pure, as far as this is possible. Let him get along with little; let him keep his passions mortified and his body, as far as possible, like a spiritual body. All this and much more does the holy body of Christ deserve, which, like precious liqueur ought not be placed in any vessel but one which is likewise precious. What more shall I say? Since the priest is called an "angel," and the angels in heaven and around the altar tremble in reverence for the Son of God, great is the obligation that the poor priest has of celebrating well these divine mysteries.

Purity of Heart

The priest has many clear motives for looking at himself to be sure that he is well vested and may appear pleasing and beautiful in the eyes of God. His eyes should not be closed lest he hear that terrible sentence, *Friend, how did you come in here not having on a wedding garment?*(Mt 22:12).[43] Then with hands and feet bound, they will cast him into the outer darkness, because he loved the interior darkness. He did not want to look at the light that could manifest his faults and show him his obligations so that he might fulfill them. Let him look at himself and look at himself again, and let him, like the saints, beg a special grace of the Holy Spirit for this. Whatever faults he is aware of in himself, let him cleanse them with an abundance of tears. It was to signify this that God commanded in the Old Law that before entering to offer sacrifice, the priests should wash their hands and feet in a large vessel full of water placed at the entrance of the temple. To remind her priests of the need for such purification with an abundance of tears, even with regard to very small things, the Church ordained that before proceeding to the consecration of the Most Holy Body of Jesus Christ, the priests should wash the tips of their fingers. This manifests what St. Dionysius said, that *as it behooves a priest to confect the celestial sacraments with clean hands, it is right for him to approach the holy mysteries with interior purity.* He also says that, by this ablution, *he attains the greatest cleanness, that having been constituted in the most chaste habit of divine goodness, he may proceed also according to the divine image of goodness, free and liberated from all mortal affection, and thus pass over into the hope of God.* [44]

What is this that we are hearing? Who will manage to possess such a superhuman purity, imitating that of God Himself, which makes man pass into unity with the spirit of God, so that, with sufficient preparation, he might deal with Him as like with like and holy with holy?

Priestly Humility

In conclusion, this priestly office demands things so sublime that there have been many saints who, terrified by its radiance, have not dared to take on such a dignity. They have chosen to reverence it as an honorable Lady but not to take it as spouse.

St. Mark was one of those. By cutting off his thumb, he tried to escape the heavy responsibility of this office. There were many Fathers in the desert of venerable age, surpassing holiness, and marvelous miracles, who seeing the desire to make them priests, fled from their monasteries and went as pilgrims in foreign lands. They considered well spent any labor at all in order to flee the dangerous risk run by the unworthy man who takes on such a high dignity.

Blessed Saint Martin left the company of the bishop, St. Hilary, who wanted to ordain him a deacon. Saint Jerome tells of another who had to be bound hand and foot in order to ordain him.

There is no reason to leave the blessed Saint Francis out of this list. Completely against his will and constrained by obedience, he was ordained a deacon. Once he was in that rank, many tried to persuade him to go on to be ordained to say Mass. With much fear and affliction, Francis commended himself to Our Lord, imploring Him to show His holy will so that he could fulfill it. As he was going along the road thinking about this matter, and persevering in asking light from the Lord, an angel appeared to him. He held a flask in his hand, clear and transparent as crystal and full of clear and shining liqueur. The angel said these words to him: "As clear as this liqueur and this glass, must the soul of the priest be." Considering that brilliance and great purity, and comparing it with the disposition of his soul, it seemed to Francis that his purity was insufficient to celebrate a Mass. This remained so impressed upon his soul, so that never again, however much he was invited, was it possible to succeed in getting him to be ordained a priest.

4.

Renewal of the Priesthood

The Call to Renewal

Oh, what a great thing it would be not to go any further and not to flee the beauty of this holy mountain, but to remain here to consider the great esteem these men had for the sacred honor of the priesthood! Some had such reverence that, as we have said, they did not dare to take it on. Others took it on through pure obedience to God and with sufficient signs from Him that He was commanding it. As men called by Him and at the disposition of His mercy, they handled His holy body and blood with great fear and trembling, with an abundance of tears and contrition, and with ardent love. They held the time of Mass in such high regard that they ordered their whole lives to acquiring the purity and true sanctity needed to be there, as they should. Even if they were rich in sanctity, they considered themselves lacking, for they saw the truth that no sanctity, however great, exceeds or equals the high dignity of the priesthood.

But alas! We are compelled to take our eyes from those who thus reverenced this holy office and lower them to look at others, the sight of whom gives pain as much as the other sight gave consolation. It is like descending from heaven to hell.

Jeremiah asked for a fountain of tears so that he could weep day and night for the dead of his city. Such a fountain could be put to good use here, and with even greater reason (Jer 9:1). For he mourned the death of the body which may have been ordered to the salvation of the soul. But those now living are dead in soul, and the reason for this is yet more sorrowful: They have despised God and mistreated Him in His own divine person. This is what we do and are if we are bad priests. We treat the Lord at the altar in such a way that no sorrow in itself is sufficient to match such a great sin, committed in such a holy time, work, and place.

May You be forever blessed! Your immense goodness compelled You to descend from heaven to earth. After You announced the way of heaven with many labors and did many favors, this same goodness of Yours that brought You from heaven, compelled You to mount the cross. There, having suffered great torments, You lost Your life, so that, by Your dying, we would regain the life that we had lost through the sin of Adam (cf Rm 5:17) and by our own sins. Seeing the great signs of love that You showed exteriorly, we would know the great fire of love for us that was burning within Your heart. Being loved, we would love You; distrusting the distrust that our sins cause us, we would trust in the mercy of the one who thus handed Himself over for our healing. You knew, Lord, the hardness of our hearts and how soon they forget the favors already received. Therefore, You magnified Your unbounded love and wonderfully ordained how, even though You went to heaven, You would be here with us. You did this by giving power to priests so that they might call You with the words of consecration, and You Yourself would come in person into their hands and be there really present. Thus, we are participants in the good things You gained by Your Passion, and we remember it with profound gratitude and consolation, loving and obeying the one that did such a great work, which was to give His life for us.

The Priest as a Sign of Christ

This was the Lord's intention, and the Mass is a representation of his sacred Passion in this way. The priest, in consecrating and in wearing the sacred vestments, represents the Lord in His Passion and death. He also represents Him in the meekness with which He suffered and in His obedience even to death on the cross, in the purity of His chastity and in the depth of His humility. He represents Him in the fire of the love which would make the priest intercede for all with the deepest sighs and offer himself to suffering and death for their healing, if the Lord should want to accept him. Finally, he has to be such a true representation that the priest is transformed into Christ, and, as St. Dionysius puts it, becomes *in one likeness*.[45] Being so conformed, there are not two, but what St. Paul says is fulfilled: *whoever clings to God, is one spirit with Him* (1 Cor 6:17). This is the representation of the sacred Passion that takes place in the Mass. This is what it means for the priest to have his arms extended in the form of a cross and to raise and lower them. It is the meaning of the vestments and everything else. With such a representation as this, the Eternal Father is very pleased, and the Son of God is well treated and served.

To Crucify Christ Again?

But alas, what sorrow! The representation has been turned into the contrary. For the bad priest does not represent Christ our Lord, except in words and in exterior things; but in his customs and behavior, he represents those who caused Christ's death and bitter passion. The first representation is something pleasing; the second is very lamentable. Oh Eternal King, You fulfilled the painful obedience of Your laborious life and death on the cross that the Father placed as our remedy. You rose in a glorious body and ascended to heaven in glorious triumph over death and sin. You are seated at the right hand of the Father and are reverenced, praised, and loved by the angels and saints who are in heaven. Who would think that there remained to You, Lord, anything upon the earth, in which Your very divine Person would be despised and treated as You were in Your Passion?

On Holy Thursday night, when the Lord was dining with His disciples, and Judas was with them, the Lord said of one of them, *Behold, the hand of him who betrays Me is with Me on the table* (Lk 22:21).[46] According to Bede,[47] the Lord says the same to the angels when He is on the altar in the hands of a bad priest. If the other Judas gave him a kiss pretending a false peace, the same is not lacking here. How bad the taste and how bitter the kisses which the bad priest gives You at the altar! Is it not right that You say to him what You said to the other: *Judas, do you betray the Son of man with a kiss?*(Lk 22:48).[48] The kiss is a sign of peace and of interior love, that hearts are joined together and that the will is one. Why, bad priest, do you give a kiss of peace exteriorly, while interiorly you are so lacking in conformity with the will of Christ? To satisfy your passions, you wage cruel war against Him and make yourself one of those, and even worse than them *who speak peace with their neighbor, but evils are in their hearts* (Ps 27:3m).[49] Oh

---

[m] Once again, in the older version of the Douay-Rheims and in the Latin Vulgate, this can be found in Psalm 27, whereas the Revised Standard version

what a distance and what a difference there is between the defilement of such a mouth and the purity which is needed to give the kiss of peace to the most pure Lord, the lover and author of purity itself. Alas, what sorrow! With the same lips that once and many times have united with and kissed a wicked woman, with those same lips, the Son of God is sacrilegiously kissed. Thus, He is, as Bede said, handed over, not to the executioners, as Judas did, but to filthy and sinful members.

The Sense of Sin

What does darkness have to do with light and Belial with Christ? *What do you have to do with women*—says St. Jerome—*you who converse at the altar with Christ?*[50] If someone had the eyes of an eagle so that he could see clearly the purity of Christ and the ugliness of indecent lust, I believe the man would fall dead from sorrow and fright at the sight of a dishonorable man daring to touch, kiss, and receive Christ, the source of all purity. In the Passion, His enemies looked at Him with terrible eyes; here He is looked at with indecent eyes, overfed to the point where they could not be more indecent in looking at what they ought not. Why should one who has embraced a mistress be joined with Christ in an embrace, more distasteful to Him than when His arms were bound and He was tied to the pillar and beaten in the house of Pilate? What will Christ say of the hands with which the bad priest touches Him? As we have said, the Lord commanded in the Law that the priest who had touched a dead bird or animal could not go to the altar to touch the sacrifices that were nothing but other animals.

These are hands bloodstained with evil works, hands that have touched unclean things that You, Lord, know. They are hands suitable for striking the Lord and touching Him unworthily. They wound Him more and cause more sorrow to His soul, if He were

---

has this as Psalm 28.

able to suffer, than the blows of the executioner caused to His most holy face. Concerning this, St. Bernard is filled with fear saying, *They dare to touch the sacred flesh of the immaculate lamb and to dip into the blood of the Savior the wicked hands which a short time before—alas!—touched the flesh of prostititues.*[51] The same saint says that there were many such priests. It would be right if, aware of their unworthiness, they would wash it away with tears at the altar. But there is nothing of this. Rather, with bold temerity, they proceed forth, even to the point of opening their mouths to receive the Lord.

Sin in the Priest

Oh, Eternal King! What do You feel, what do You say, what do You think when You see over You a mouth which is defiled, dark, and bloodied, opened to consume you, as a wolf swallows a lamb? But are we not asking Him something, which He foresaw many years before He became man? He spoke then and complained about what is happening now: *They have opened their mouths against Me, as a lion ravening and roaring* (Ps 21:14[n]).[52] The mouth of the bad priest is a more terrible lion for the soul of the Son of God than those angry priests and cruel executioners were for His sacred body, when they opened their mouths wanting to tear Him to pieces.

The Lord suffers and is silent like a gentle lamb. This is because He came not to judge the world but to do penance for our sins. When He was insulted and called a Samaritan and possessed, He did not avenge Himself, but responded, *I do not seek My honor, but there is one who seeks it and judges* (Jn 8:50).[53] Thus, even if He sees Himself consumed by so unworthy a mouth, He suffers and is silent. He remits the case to His Father, complaining of this Judas as He complained of the other, saying, *God, be not silent,*

---

[n] The original version of the Douay-Rheims Catholic Bible (which follows the Latin Vulgate) shows this as Psalm 21:14, whereas the RSV translation has it as Psalm 22:14.

for the mouth of the wicked and the mouth of the deceitful is opened against Me (Ps 108:2o).[54] The more Christ is silent, the louder, *as a woman in labor* (Is 42:14),[55] will His Father speak, severely punishing such a sinner who opened his mouth to consume His Only Begotten Son. A mouth defiled by lust and gluttony, a tongue which has dealt with lies, boasting, angry and indecent words, and has bitten and eaten the flesh of its neighbors, by speaking evil of them and ruining their reputations! Concerning such, Scripture says that there are people who have their teeth as arms and a sharp arrow and that their tongue is a sharp knife and an arrow which wounds (cf. Ps 56:5p). With those teeth and that tongue, the bad priest flays and chews his neighbor to pieces. His mouth is then left stained with the blood of his neighbor that he has drunk, like a dog in a butcher's shop that drinks the blood of the animals slaughtered there. With his mouth stained with the blood of his neighbor, an adopted child of God, the Father of the one whose blood he has in his mouth, he goes to the altar to receive Jesus Christ.

Oh what a disgusting thing for a Father who loves His children so much! But, in the end, a bad priest makes Him suffer this hard thing. Taking Christ in his mouth, he places Him in a breast which causes Him more grief than the very cross upon which He was placed. There Christ hung, as St. Augustine says,[56] by His own will and with much joy, because through that rough bed, our souls would be cleansed from our sins, and He would remain in them, pure within the pure. But now He is placed within a breast that is not much different from hell, for the presence of sins is the principal characteristic of hell. Christ cannot be without great sorrow—if He were able to suffer now—at seeing His labors lost—His blood poured out in vain for that priest. Babylonia has been treated but not healed (Jer 51:9). The Lord cannot suffer now and sorrow has no place in Him. It did have a place during

---

o In the RSV translation, this would be Psalm 109.

p This would be Psalm 57 in the RSV translation.

His mortal life, and He knew the insults that would be directed at Him. These caused grave bitterness to His soul because they were such grave sins.

Loss of the Fear of God

The bad priest, having consecrated Christ and received Him, not in a new tomb, but in the pit where infernal swine wallow, finishes his Mass, said very quickly, and goes off to his affairs. He returns to his sins, without respect, fear, or shame for the betrayal of the Lord. His shamelessness is like that of Judas. Neither respect for the presence of the Lord nor the loyalty owed to those who eat together at the same table, nor the threats or gentle words of the Lord, moved him to repentance and consciousness of his sin. Receiving Him in his breast like the other apostles, did not move him either. None of these things prevented him from leaving the presence of the Lord to put into effect the wickedness of his heart.[57]

Such shamelessness, says St. Bernard, in speaking of the same subject, is a grave thing. Because when man becomes hardened and is not afraid, and neither fears nor trembles, then the situation is already desperate. "Whoever is conscious of these things himself is to all, just as he who does justice is not afraid to present himself to the Divine Face; just as the servant enters and exits, greets the Teacher, bends the knee, kisses with a sacrilegious kiss, even acts slyly before God, in such a way that his iniquity unto hatred is discovered: he is clearly hateful to God, his temerity is scandalous, and his shamelessness is to be cursed." They have lost the fear of God and shame before men, and therefore their misery is greater and the remedy more difficult. As Saint Chrysostom says, "If lay people sin, they are easily corrected, but if clerics commit sin, they prove to be incapable of correction."[58]

It is a sad thing that a sinner and a villain, upon hearing a sermon, tremble at a threat from God. They have some reverence for the temple of God, the altar, and the things of God. But the priest has lost fear, with much contact. He does not have love nor does he know what it is. What is left, before he is like Judas in life and death? He is very displeasing in the eyes of God, and his blindness is profound. Thus, it seems to him that even if he has committed a sin of the flesh the night before, he can, without sorrow or purpose of a new life or leaving the occasions of sin, be reconciled. (Alas! Many have their prostitute in their house and then return to her...). With this confession and absolution received from another *who is under the same condemnation*, he dares to return to the altar and to mistreat the Son of God. What will become of these men? *A man who has violated the law of Moses dies without any mercy at the testimony of two or three witnesses. How much more do you think he deserves worse, who has trodden underfoot the Son of God and esteemed the blood of the covenant unclean, by which he was sanctified, and offered an affront to the Spirit of grace? For we know Him who said, 'Vengeance belongs to me, and I will repay.' And again, 'The Lord will judge his people.'*[59] With what judgment He then declares it, saying, *It is a fearful thing to fall into the hands of the living God!* (Heb 10:28-31).

A Possible Failure

The judgment of the priest has to be different because his dignity is different.

He holds a celestial office; he has become an angel of the Lord of hosts. As an angel he is either elected or condemned. When depravity is found among the angels, it is necessary that a stricter and more inexorable judgment be passed than that among humans.[60] In saying this, St. Bernard differentiates the judgment and punishment of priests from that of the common people. He compares that of priests with the judgment and punishment of the demons. Oh, woe to you, says the same saint, against the unworthy man who procures the priesthood. *Where are you going? Don't you know that a fall from a higher stage is more serious? Nor indeed will you fall slowly but like a lightning bolt with fierce impetus. Like another Satan, you will suddenly be cast down.*[61] Thus Satan fell; thus Judas died; and thus die many others who are like them. Some priests die suddenly without being able to make their confession or to speak; others die obstinate and without hope, and even if they are able to confess, they do not want to; others die blaspheming and spitting on the cross, by the just judgment of God. Many of them die with their wicked company in their house, and at times, even at their bedside. The most just justice of God is that the one who trampled on the Son of God should be punished with eternal torments. He who tramples upon Him, as the *Glosa* says, is the one *who sins without fear or penitence and who unworthily receives communion.*[62] The bad priest is capable of both things, and a third besides, which is to celebrate the Mass unworthily. This tarnishes—as far as it can—the most pure blood of Christ in which the priest was sanctified when his sins were pardoned by receiving the sacraments properly. It also offends the Holy Spirit that was poured out upon him and gave him grace in holy baptism and bestowed on him the power to be able to consecrate. By a profane life and a betrayal like that of Judas, the priest shows grave disrespect and insult toward the Father, the Son, and the Holy Spirit. With complete justice, he dies in such a way that there is neither contrition in his heart nor confession unto salvation on his lips. It was thus that the Judas died, bursting open instead of breathing forth his spirit through his mouth, as others do.

Suffering in Union with Christ

Will no one suffer at such great misery? Some officials of God, exalted to so high an honor that they have many times held in their hands the one reverenced by the angels, descend from such a height and prosperity to the torments of hell. There, in torments graver than those of the others, they are perpetual slaves of the demons, whom they were commanding here. King Saul complains, *There is no one who sorrows for me.*[63] The Son of God complained on the cross that there was no one to console him. He complains now, and very seriously and justly, that there is no one who cares for His honor and puts it in its proper place. Let those who can apply a remedy for this, each in his own way, be moved at the very just complaint of the Son of God and at the sad condemnation of so many priests. Let them be moved with compassion for the evils that come to the Christian people through this sin. No heart that has even a little knowledge of God, can bear such great contempt for Jesus Christ, such perdition of souls, such evils of various kinds. And you, Lord, Eternal Father of your Only Begotten Son, You who protect Your honor, *will You refrain Yourself, Lord? Will You keep silence and afflict us vehemently?* (Is 64:12).⁶⁴ Speak, Lord, through Your mercy, sending the Holy Spirit into the hearts of those who can remedy this situation. Grant them Your grace so that they may succeed in getting the work done.

The Sorrow of the Church

Someone here may think that these evils of the clergy that we are recounting are an exaggeration or untrue. I wish it were so. But whoever wants to be informed of what is happening and, with the prophet Ezekiel, to dig this miserable wall (cf. Ez 8:8), will see great abominations in this Babylon. They will be such as to move him to greater compassion and dismay than the perdition of the other earthly Babylon moved the prophet Isaiah (Is 21). If he does not even want to descend to touch such filthy mire with his hands, let him consider people who from the time they were boys, were brought up without obedience, without enclosure, without devotion, and with base companions. By day and by night, they went wherever they wanted, taking with them the inclinations they inherited from Adam, with no restraint and no one near at hand to go with them. In short, they lived with the misery of their appetites, and in the time of the ardor of youth, with many occasions for evil, they lacked the resources necessary to emerge victorious against such strong enemies. A burden has been cast upon them that would make the shoulders of angels tremble. It demands purity of body and soul, practiced for many years. All of this they lack; all that is contrary to it they have, almost converted into nature by long custom. What fruits should be expected from such bad roots (unless God works a miracle or almost a miracle), but the sad and bitter fruits which our eyes see, which set on edge the teeth of Mother Church? For *a foolish son is the sorrow of his mother* (Prv 10:1).[65]

The life of the priest should be such that he is free of mortal sin from his baptism. St. Paul meant this when he said that the one who is going to be a priest has to be *without offense* (Ti 1:6-7). As St. Jerome says, it is not enough that, if he has sinned, he has wept for it, but it is required that he has not committed sin.[66] This is not unreasonable, for the divine Scriptures and the saints regard mortal sin after becoming a child of God in holy baptism as very serious among the laity, and they speak of it with great emphasis. With how much greater reason is this purity and loyalty demanded of one chosen to be a reliquary of God and to have familiar dealings with Him, dealings that cannot be entrusted to one who has been a traitor to the Lord!

Lack of a Sense of the Church

People who act in this way are ordinarily poor village priests whose need for bodily food makes them frequent this divine mystery. There are others of higher station who are in no way enthusiastic about belonging to the Church. They do not long for that blessed contract there is between God and the priest, and they do not esteem it much, because being a priest does not, by itself, fill the cavity of their earthly desires. If these men enter the service of the Church, it is not because they choose to be lowly in the house of the Lord rather than rich in the world. If a good arrangement for marriage were offered to them, they would choose that. They choose the service of the Church, because it offers them greater material for their riches and comfort than in the world. Having entered with this end in view, they afterwards relish little or very little saying a Mass. If they do say it, it is because the stipend obliges them to it, or so as not to be conspicuous as bad Christians. Thus, they say Mass a few times and with tepidity. Since they do not esteem the Mass and do not possess the holiness or preparation fitting for it, they do not like doing it. Those who think they are better prepared to say Mass, with great difficulty have the disposition to receive communion well, as lay people do. But they do not know by experience the intense prayer demanded of them for the people and for the world, and they do not have the sanctity that the priestly office demands. The one who does this is highly esteemed, because people think that a rich and important person saying Mass in that manner is a great feat, and that as such, he must be esteemed and thanked. They speak the truth if they are comparing such priests with others of their qualities who say Mass while their lives are indecent, and publicly indecent, and with no one able to remedy it. But the just judgment of God will judge each one for himself, and will not justify the smaller fault because there is another greater.

A Distressing Situation

All this makes it clear how weak the Church is in this very important area of her life, the priesthood. How deformed her face is, how blind her eyes, how mute her tongue, and how little succor of prayer the Church receives from those who have such prayer as their office and obligation. To the contrary, such men need the succor of the prayers of others to oppose the wrath of God so that He may not punish them. Thus, according to Ezekiel (Ez 22:30-31), the Lord searches for a man who may resist His wrath and oppose Him on behalf of the people. Since He does not find him, He pours out his indignation over the people, according to what we read, or rather, experience in our scourges, more than in our books themselves. Even if there are some priests who carry out their office fairly well, even these lack the grandeur that this dignity demands. Moreover, they are very few in comparison with the bad ones so that the smaller part is surpassed by the larger part.

5.

Parish Priests

The Dignity and Sanctity of the Pastor

Many things are required to fulfill well the obligation of the office of pastor of souls. Looking at the priestly dignity attached to the office, it is fitting to have fervent and efficacious prayer, and also sanctity, according to what has been said above. All of this will be more advantageous in the parish priest in light of the greater and more particular obligation he has of giving good example to his parishioners and interceding for them before the divine majesty. He must do this with the affection of a father and a mother for their children, since he is called father of his parishioners. The many diverse occupations that his office demands indicate how much the priest needs prayer. It is not easy to have prayer and devotion in the midst of many occupations, even if they are good. For the same reason, it becomes necessary that his sanctity be very firm. For there are in his office many occasions for losing sanctity, as reason and experience show. St. John Chrysostom ponders this,[67] and St. Augustine is amazed that those in this office have any virtue left standing.[68]

Sanctification in the Ministry

Apart from the obligation he has to be a good priest and to keep watch over his own conscience, the parish priest also has the office of helping and teaching the souls of the faithful. As St. Gregory says, this requires no less sanctity than to offer the holy sacrifice of the altar.[69] Pondering this, St. Chrysostom remarks that the one entrusted with souls has been entrusted with the Mystical Body of Jesus Christ, so that he might care for it and strengthen it. He must make it beautiful with such virtues that it may be worthy of being called the body of such a head as Jesus Christ is.[70] St. Paul says the same, in a sentence in these words: *For I have espoused you to one husband, that I may present you as a chaste virgin to Christ* (2 Cor 11:2).[71] It is a great task for a man to be charged with teaching the spouse of such a great king, instructing her in customs that will give joy to the king. This is especially so, since she is weak in virtue, without much prudence, and not very obedient to her mentor.

Thus, the Lord commands the pastors of the rational sheep that they strengthen what is weak and heal what is sick, that they bind up what is broken and bring back the outcast, and that they seek the lost (cf Ez 34:4). For this, many and very good qualities are necessary. With reason did St. Gregory say that *the direction of souls is the art of arts*.[72] Much prudence is needed to know how to take medicine to such diverse people and to give what is suitable to each one. A lot of patience is needed to suffer the importunities of sheep, both wise and unwise. May God give him, as He gave to Jeremiah, a face as strong as diamond and flint[73] so that he may not be overcome by the threats and evil deeds of those who do not want to be drawn away from their sins or reprimanded for them, and do not want priests to carry out their office. It is good to be like the prophet who says, *I am filled with the strength of the Lord, that I might declare to Jacob his sin* (Mi 3:8).[74] Fortitude is very necessary for those who hold public offices, but rarely possessed, because there are few untouched, more or less, by the desire to please their friends and the fear of displeasing their enemies.

Preaching and Study

The doctor must have knowledge of medicine in order to teach. What the pastor has to teach is the faith and Christian customs. In the beginning of the Church, it was the office of the deacon to catechize those who would become Christians, instructing them in the articles of the faith and purging them of the evil and worldly customs in which they had been raised as Gentiles. After they were baptized, it was the responsibility of the priest to enlighten them in the knowledge of the holy sacraments, as St. Dionysius says,[75] and to instruct them with wise admonitions for life, as Pope St. Clement said.[76] But now that the office of deacons has ceased[q], it is the responsibility of the priest to teach the parishioners what they need to know to work for their salvation. In order that this be done fruitfully, the priest must be fairly learned in the law of God contained in His Sacred Scriptures, for

---

[q] Although apparently the permanent diaconate was no longer in use at the time of St. John of Avila, it's use was restored in the Latin rite of the Catholic Church after the Second Vatican Council, in which *Lumen Gentium* 29, approved this future possibility. The possibility became a reality on June 18, 1967, the feast of St. Ephraim, a deacon, when Pope Paul VI published his apostolic letter, *Sacrum Diaconatus Ordinem*, permitting Episcopal conferences to request this ordination to the permanent diaconate from the Holy See.

in them is found what is useful for bringing about these effects. As St. Paul says, *All Scripture, inspired by God, is profitable to teach, to reprove, to correct, to instruct in justice* (2 Tm 3:16). Thus, it is fitting that the parish priest should know Sacred Scripture—if not the difficult parts, then at least what is simple and straightforward.

The holy doctors were men enlightened by God and experienced in the care of spiritual infirmities. They have written many things useful for the diagnosis and healing of such infirmities, and many salutary prescriptions to preserve the health arrived at and to teach and persuade the people in the way of God. Therefore, it is good that the priest be well read in the moral teaching of the saints. Without it, he will not understand the Scriptures with certainty. He will also make many errors in the care of souls through not making use of the advice of the physicians God gave us.

Orientation and Direction

The priest is not only a physician and teacher; he is also a judge. To give sentences by which, in conformity with God's will, he opens and closes the kingdom to those in his charge, it is suitable for him also to have knowledge of particular things of conscience, treated in Councils, Canon Law, and summaries by men learned in this field. To fulfill his obligations well, much favor from the Lord is necessary and much diligence on the part of the curate. For, as the saints say, the same conditions that the Apostle demands of one who would be a good bishop, are demanded of one who would perform well the office of pastor, even if not with the same degree of perfection.

The office of watchman is also suitable for the priest, and for this reason, St. Paul called the priests of Ephesus bishops (cf Acts 20:28; 1 Tm 3; Ti 1:5f). They are also called pastors, and against them are directed the threats of the Lord against the shepherds who do not do what they should. Particularly, the apostle St. Peter speaks to them saying, *Let the elders who are among you* ...[77] (Acts

20:17, 28; cf Eph 4:11); or, according to the Greek, *presbyteros*, etc. In part, these run a greater risk than the bishops themselves do, because they have closer dealings with persons of different kinds. The closer the relationships are, the more vehement are the dangers they cause. For this reason, the priest has to be very mature in every virtue. This is especially so in the use of the holy sacrament of penance, for which he needs much prudence, charity, chastity, efficacy in word and fervent prayer. Above all, it is good for the priest to have true love for our Lord Jesus Christ. This love will cause the priest to have zeal so fervent that it will consume his heart with pain that God is offended. He will try to remove such offenses, so that God may be as honored and reverenced exteriorly in divine worship as interiorly in his heart. Toward God he has the heart of a faithful son, and toward his parishioners, the heart of a true father and a true mother. Christian priests should be such that they do not need someone else to watch out for their souls because, as St. Gregory says, *Those for whom help from others is still necessary, are not to be promoted to the position of helping others.*[78]

6.

Confessors

The Ministry of Confession

The ministry of physician of souls, which is incumbent upon the priest, is very close to that of confessors, even if they are not parish priests. This ministry must be carried out well. It is so important for the good of the Church, for if there were good confessors, a large part of the road toward reform of the Church would be covered. Sooner or later, all the faithful go to confession. If they should fall into the hands of ministers who have the art of treating souls and zeal for their salvation, it is certain that the Christian people would walk at a very different pace than they are now walking.

The qualities the confessor must have, whether he is a parish priest or not, are set forth in the Clementine *Dudum de sepulturis* in these words: *Let them take care to choose persons who are able, suitable, of proven character, discreet, modest, and skillful to carry out such a salutary ministry and office.*[79] In this holy sacrament, not only are infirm souls cured, but the dead are raised. As St. Bernard says, *The revival of the soul is a great sacrament.*[80] Many times it turns out to be quite difficult to place the penitent in a reasonable disposition, so that he may be ready for the fruit of sacramental absolution. Therefore, the confessor needs much prudence, patience, and above all, charity, which make him groan and pray to the Lord and do penance, so that through his ministry he may give light and grace to his penitent. To carry out this office well, the Clementine decretal very justly requires the conditions already mentioned, and none of them is excessive.

Renewal

A comparison of the conditions required for good use of the ministry of parish priests and confessors, with the conditions of those who now exercise these ministries, causes deep sorrow. Amazingly, there may be someone who has them all. But many lack most of them, and others lack all of them.

The good life required to exercise this ministry has been so lacking that it has been necessary to bring to the Inquisition things that happen between confessors and penitents. This has not been without cause. For experience has shown that such a crowd of people goes to bring charges about this to the judges of the faith, as usually are found at a great solemnity or great jubilee in a land of devout people. The judges have been informed of very ugly things, unworthy of being mentioned, and sufficient to provoke the wrath of God and to punish His people with severe blows.

From this, it is possible to deduce the grave errors and intolerable havoc that such ministers have caused in souls, and the less they come forth to exterior judgment, so that they can be cured, the more dangerous they are.

The Root of the Evil

If we consider the knowledge that these ministers are supposed to have, we have to say that there is none, as can be seen even by the blind. The prelates see this very thing. But if someone asks why they consent to such ministers, they respond, "You give us better ones and we will take them. We do not have others; we take the least bad ones of those we find." It appears as if the prelates have no obligation to educate good ministers (concerning which we will speak of later), and things being as they are, it is no wonder that we have the ministers we have. They have no formation and education and no preparation to attain virtue. With the same freedom as they lived before they were ordained, they live after they are ordained. Where are they going to be taught cases of conscience and of moral conscience? There is no instruction in such things in the seven or more universities in the kingdoms of Castile. For this purpose, it is of little benefit that they instruct in Theology and Canon Law, for those who exercise the offices of parish priest and confessor are unwilling to undertake such long studies. Many lack the possibility of maintaining themselves in these universities, and if someone does have the means, he does not want to undertake the labors. If he does want to undertake the labors and comes out [of the university], he seeks to fly to greater gains. He does not want to lower himself to the work of parish priests and of the confessional, unless it is to claim for himself some parish with a fat stipend, with as little fruit for the parishioners as comes from others who have no learning. In this way, just as Our Lord Jesus Christ in the Sacrament of the altar is treated most unworthily by His ministers, so His holy Mystical Body, which is the souls of the faithful, is badly shattered and deformed through the fault of evil ministers. Those who were supposed to be shepherds turn themselves into wolves and make carnage of the souls of those they were supposed to bring to life. They take care of their own comfort and interests and give of themselves very little for the benefit of their sheep. *And they took care of the wound of the daughter of my people disgracefully, saying, 'Peace, peace' and there was no peace* (Jer 6:14).[81] They absolve one whom God does not absolve and with that *they strengthen the hands of the most wicked* (Jer 23:14).[82] Thus, the office of caring for souls in confession and outside it, is carried out without fruit and provokes the wrath of God against His people.

Conciliar Doctrine

The Holy Council of Trent was made aware of this evil. As one remedy for it, the Council commanded that no one be ordained to say Mass if he did not first know how to administer well the sacraments of the Church, especially that of penance.[83] The Council was moved to this by being informed that in some parts there was instruction in particular cases of conscience, but that it was not possible to complete the work with the priests who were attending the instructions. If they did attend, they were not studying, and they were putting such impediments to one thing and another, that they wearied the instructor and the prelate. These men who so abhor learning, being in orders, are greedy for receiving priestly ordination. Knowing that they cannot achieve it if they do not study first, they subject themselves to study in order to go out with that printed piece of paper.

But the prelates do not observe what has been decreed in such a holy manner, as a thing in which the Holy Spirit intervened. It must be because, in most places, there is no one who instructs in cases of conscience. So that it may not cost them some money to hire someone to give instruction concerning these cases, they ordain someone who does not know them, and from such men as these come confessors and parish priests.

Unfulfilled Conciliar Decrees

With the same end in view, the Council also commanded that no priest, secular or religious, could hear confessions if he were not examined by the Ordinary.[84] This is still not kept, or so badly kept, that things are as they were at the beginning. Then they were so bad, among secular clerics as among many religious, including even the mendicants, that the situation was intolerable because of the grave damage to souls that followed, as much through the ignorance of the confessors as through their evil lives. For the evils that have been verified in these affairs have pertained to both these things.

7.

Preachers

Proclamation of the Word

The office of the preachers of the Word of God is compared to many temporal things which give us clues through which we may know the grandeur of this ministry. They are called "heavens" because as the material heavens manifest the glory of God, the preachers more clearly preach the perfections of God (Rm 10:18). They are people set aside to glorify the Lord. Isaiah's words can be applied to them. *They are a garden for the Lord, for His glorification* (Is 61:3);[85] and in another place: *I have created this people for Myself; they will tell forth My praise* (Is 43:21).[86]

Blessed office, through which God is magnified in human hearts and esteemed as worthy of being feared, reverenced and loved! Moreover, because God in His goodness regards doing good to men as an honor and wants to show His greatness, He gives people a remedy for their salvation. He takes these preachers as a means to save men, because He wants them to be instruments of His glory. Thus, of those "heavens" is understood what the Lord said through Isaiah, *as rain and snow descend* (Is 55:10). The Word of the Lord in the mouth of His preachers waters the dryness of souls like rain coming down from heaven. Inebriated with the gentle love of the Lord, it makes them bring forth fruit in good works. By experience, we know that where the Word of God is preached, people are different than where it is not. It is just as the earth that receives rain and is fertile is different from the dry earth, which gives forth thorns and thistles instead of fruit. But the earth that has received rain also needs to be helped by the heat of the sun, as well as by the moisture. Therefore, the preachers are also compared to the sun because by the heat and fire of God's Word, they produce fruit in souls that is beneficial for the one who produces it, and ripe and delicious to the Lord. By illuminating the understanding, they give the knowledge of God and teach the way to heaven, illuminating the hindrances that can be found along the path.

Christ, the Word of God

So as not to go into detail about everything that should be said, we summarize. The Word that descended from heaven to this world came as a man. As true sun and true light, He enlightened the earth with His teaching and example. He inundated it, consoling it and giving it joy. He gave sight to the blind, hearing to the deaf, and health to those infirm with many and great infirmities. He even raised the dead. Afterwards, He gave his life on the cross, an action completely sufficient to win for men the blessed life that has no end.

The Word Now Present in the Church

But all the goods which the Uncreated Word of God worked in the bodies of men and those which He gained for souls through His passion, He works and effects through His Word, which He left here. With this Word, He enlightens our ignorance, enkindles our tepidity, mortifies our passions, and, what is more, raises up the souls that are dead, a greater work than to create heaven and earth. With this Word, the Lord wounds and gives health, puts to death and gives life, places in hell and draws out of it, humiliates and exalts, because with fear of His justice, He makes the sinner tremble and to know himself worthy of hell. With the gentleness of His words, promising mercy to penitents, He consoles the one who weeps, raises up the fallen, and makes confident the one who was at the point of despair. Not only does He free from death, but He also gives sustenance for life, for His Word is the sustenance of the soul. It is water with which it cleanses itself, fire with which it warms itself, arms for fighting, a bed for resting, and light from above so as not to wander. Finally, just as the Uncreated Word of God has power for all things, so is His Word in…[r]

---

[r] Here St. John of Avila stops abruptly and left the book unfinished.

BULL OF CANONIZATION

✠

Bull of Pope Paul VI in which the honors of the saints are decreed on Blessed John of Ávila. 31st of May of 1970.

Paul, Bishop, servant of the Servants of God for perpetual memory

Introduction

The most holy words of Christ, "Go into the whole world and proclaim the gospel to every creature. Whoever believes and is baptized will be saved; whoever does not believe will be condemned" (Mk 16:15-16), clearly indicate that the salvation of man relies above all on the preaching of the Bishops, successors of the Apostles and also on the preaching of those who, with them, participate in that most holy mystery, that is to say, the Priests. And this in reality is the reason for which the Church has placed her trust above all in the Bishops and Priests, in difficult times as well as in good times.

The consciousness of priestly dignity and the reform of customs, motives for canonization

For the most part, since the College of our Venerable Brothers, Bishops of Spain, in their own name, in the name of the clergy and of the whole nation, have asked that Blessed John of Ávila, Priest of utmost integrity and, at the same time, promoter of the Christian religion in that most noble land, be elevated by us to the number of the Saints. We, desirous in a way of augmenting the glory of such an elucidated nation, homeland of so many saints and illustrious men, and in another, judging that it ought to contribute in a favorable and joyful manner to the prosperity of the Church, after considering the case with due thought, we happily accede to their petitions and proceed in consequence.

Because if the Church, afflicted in former times by many difficulties at the surging of heresies on all parts and also at the fall of piety and discipline into a certain languidness, was strengthened above all in Spain with the virtue of this blessed man, trusts that his holiness, proclaimed by the supreme Seat of Peter, will encourage Priests, so that they, conscious of their dignity, may structure their lives according to the demands, criteria and norms of virtue. In this manner, they will illuminate the faithful as the light placed on the light post and separate them from the corruption of bad habits.

Everybody sees how much help this will contribute to the Church oppressed by the weight of those great duties that have been commended to her, and what vigor it will inspire in the way of a favorable wind so that She may be able to reach the final port.

1.

The Life of Saint John of Avila

It is our pleasure to briefly recall the life of this blessed man and to highlight his great holiness with the goal that at getting to know him, everyone may admire him and at admiring him, imitate him.

Studies and preparation to go to Mexico

John of Ávila was born in Almodóvar, Spain, on the 6th day of January of 1499, son of Alonso and Catalina Xixón, rich in temporal goods as well as in religion and faith. At that time, Spanish knights acquired much renown with their military triumph, and this influenced so that the child's character would be forged in an atmosphere of very brilliant events.

He had just turned 14 years old when he's sent to Salamanca, center of studies and of the Arts. Already at 15, and for unknown causes, he leaves the city, reintegrating himself into his home. A son of the Franciscan family, who had heard talk of his profoundly lived religion and piety, advised him to resume his interrupted studies and that, continuing his studies, be ordained a priest, for in this way, he'd served Christ in his Church more advantageously.

And so, already in Alcalá, he dedicated himself with complete effort to the study of philosophy and of sacred theology, planning in turn to go to the Indies once his studies were completed. There's no surprise that when the Bishop of Tlaxcala, Julián Garcés, was looking for missionaries to Mexico, John would joyfully accept enlisting and would then concentrate on the desires of his soul and would seek orientation.

Thus he hastened, before all else, to celebrate the Holy Mass in Almodóvar, his city of birth. Certainly at such an occasion, at the example of Christ, he served at table and clothed 12 poor persons once again. Furthermore, detaching himself from his rich patrimony, he distributed all the money he had saved among the needy, and from riches he became poor and indigent. It is the evangelical councils that gave him much strength, and he would devote his whole soul to their fulfillment.

Afterwards, he directed himself to the city of Sevilla, so that from there he would put out to sea with the end of preaching Christ in Mexico, prepared to undergo any labor in this endeavor. But things did not go according to his plan.

Apostolic mission in Andalucía

No hurricane-like force could extinguish the fire now burning in his heart. And this good servant of God traveled throughout the whole region of Andalucía in apostolic style, proclaiming the Kingdom of God; and many cities, including Alcalá de Guadaira, Lebrija, Jerez, Palma del Río, Ecija, were for him like his Galilee.

The power of his rhetoric and talent, together with a great poverty and an irreproachable innocence, penetrated and moved hearts. Many were those who by the preaching of the Truth would be captured wherever he tossed his nets.

He leaves the Inquisition, innocent and penetrated by the "Mystery of Christ"

The year 1531 takes the innocent John to the tribunal of the Inquisition of Sevilla as a suspect for heresy and is punished by imprisonment. Finally, having been interrogated and following an efficacious defense, he is liberated. Certainly, prison benefited him since among chains and shadows, he perceived the "Mystery of Chirst" with greater plenitude than he had ever known.

Córdoba and Granada; teacher of priests and of saints

Inflamed by this divine fire, John directs himself toward Córdoba and there he founds the school named "Priestly Concerns[s]", in which the formation of Priests was sought. Thus, he nourished their lives of piety in such a way that, moved by the fame and brilliance of his virtues, the priests held him as their example.

John went to Granada. There he greatly helped the Archbishop; he preached without rest; he collaborated in the college of Priests as the auxiliary to the Prelate, and he took on important charges, which he exercised in a holy way. In all, it was here in the university where he attained the name, "Teacher." This place, with divine help, converted John of God, driving him to a greater surrender to divine service; as also was the case with Francis of Borja and other illustrious men and women, in whom the Church rightly rejoices.

Foundation of the University of Baeza

In the year 1540, he founded a University in Baeza and wisely organized it. He instituted it with such norms so that it would appear clear to all that his teachings were founded on the philosophy of St. Thomas Aquinas. He would also help make the formators of youth capable for the apostolate with the necessary science and doctrine. Likewise, he made sure that together with the University, colleges and faculties would be erected, where before all else, Christian doctrine would be expounded.

For, at that time, Pedro Guerrero, Archbishop of Granada, once his classmate in Alcalá and about to make his way to Trent to take part in the Holy Council, insistently begged him to go with him. Unable to accompany him, he composed a Memorial or statement on the reform of the Church; a Memorial that the Prelate used at the Holy Synod and which was accepted and produced many fruits. John, remaining in his homeland, dedicated himself fully to the preaching of the Word of God; and in a special way,

---

[s] "Preocupaciones Sacerdotales"

he focused on running the "School for Priests", which he had successfully founded.

Saint John of Ávila and Saint Ignatius of Loyola

In those days, the Society of Jesus, founded by Ignatius of Loyola, began to propagate throughout Spain. John and Ignatius, in complete accordance, pursued the same goals through the same means and labor. This mutual affinity soon made them friends. Not only did each one hold a high opinion of the other and recognized his merits, but they also loved and helped each other as if they belonged to the same family. Furthermore, at John's guidance, no small number of his disciples entered the Society of Jesus. Moreover, John himself would have joined such holy society had his poor health not impeded it.

If this would have been the case, Saint Ignatius, as he himself said, would have had him carried upon someone's shoulders as if he were dealing with the "Arc of the Covenant."

His last years in Montilla

Exhausted by his continuous works and vigils, he began to perceive discomforts, limitations and sicknesses. At the aggravation of these and having left the ministry of preaching out of necessity, he retired to the city of Montilla, where he lived with his coworker, Fr. Villarás. That small house, ordinary if one judges by appearances, became very noble and rich if one considers its dignity.

Writer and spiritual director

During this period, the holy man wrote magnificent works and directed many souls. He prudently composed another treatise so that the Prelate of Granada would once again use it at Trent. This advisor and constant motivator of priests sent those who were gathered in Córdoba in 1553 a small but concise treatise. In the year 1565, he in a way intervened in the Council of Toledo by means of letters and memorials. In the year 1568, this extremely prudent teacher of virtues encouraged the spirit of Teresa of Jesus, which was bothered with scruples, with his letters that openly approved the Book she had written of her life.

He died serenely on the 10th of May of 1569

Exhausted by sufferings, it was necessary for him to retire to bed, and there, resembling Christ, he was nailed to the Cross. It is known that he lived this opposition at the rhythm of the saints, and signs of virtue were so evident that he seemed to be filled with a certain divine influence to the point that his time spent in Montilla seemed like nothing but a preparation for his death. On the 10th of May, 1569 he died peacefully. His body was entombed in the religious house of the sons of the Society of Jesus. The fame of his name spread with great praise.

2.

The Holiness of Saint John of Ávila

Faithful image of Saint Paul

It is now our pleasure to briefly meditate on the valor and works of this man. First of all, John, in likeness to Paul, to whom he admirably united his lineage, temperament and ability, was truly an apostle, and as history proclaims, "a clear image of evangelical preaching" as well as "a faithful copy of the holy apostle."

Since he solely loved God, he cared about mankind with great enthusiasm and suffered for whom, surrounded by danger, he would call "children of tears." There is no doubt that everything he endeavored to do—his prayers, his assiduousness in hearing confessions, and his exhausting works—he would direct for the salvation of sinners. And if there was something he couldn't do on his own, he would make the effort to attain it by means of his writings or through his disciples, and it was done always with extraordinary and constant diligence.

Projects of reform sent to the Council of Trent

Very laudable and meritorious was the collaboration of his sharp ingenuity in the statutes, decrees and mandates of the Sacred Council of Trent: that the teaching of catechism be preserved, a task that not only he was occupied with, for which he also wrote a work titled, *Of Christian Doctrine* that would open new opportunities in catechism; that there be a firm will in the reform of clerical customs; that in the foundation of colleges, in some way similar to Seminaries, all diligence be placed; and finally, that Priests, like soldiers prepared for everything, be ready for service to their Bishops.

Friend of all and Teacher of Saints

John was the friend and father in Christ of many men of every condition—noble and humble, priest and laity—they were the consolations of his works, tasks, and sorrows. At the same time, a far-reaching friendship united him with the Saints: John of God, Francis of Borja, Peter of Alcántara, Ignatius of Loyola, John of Ribera, Thomas of Villaneueva, and Theresa of Jesus. Among them he enjoyed their great esteem, in particular, that of St. Theresa of Jesus, who deeply mourned his death.

Mystery of Christ: "Flesh, Cross, Eucharist"

The capital nucleus of his superabundant doctrine is the "Mystery of Christ", which, as we mentioned, God unveiled to him while in jail. The mystery of Christ, according to the thought of this blessed man, is summarized in the following: that God so loved man that He gave them His Only Begotten Son, whose love stood out above all else in the Incarnation, at the Cross, and in the Eucharist. The Love of God, if we are to use his same words, became "Flesh, Cross, Eucharist".

Therefore, Christians are able to participate in the goods of the Divine Redeemer and unite themselves through grace to Christ, with the head as with the remaining members. If we observe the relationship among the members, it is necessary for charity itself to give them cohesion. It doesn't escape anyone that this brilliantly insinuates the doctrine of the "Mystical Body", as subsequently was clarified by the Church. John of Avila has truly been meritorious for his doctrine.

The topic of priesthood in his writings

To the one who considers his writings and his life, it will soon arise how the subject of the priesthood occupied the highest place for John. He is convinced that Priests, by the sacred authority of orders, carry out the priesthood of Christ himself; it is suitable, for the most part, that they live in a holy manner, conscious of such a high dignity, by the very act that they ought to celebrate the Sacrament of the Eucharist with fear and trembling. It is also clear to him that the Priests, like Jesus Christ, are mediators between the people and God since it is through them that the Word of God reaches man. And since the office of the priest is a sign of God, who is Love, then it is suitable that love be spread with love. For all else, the perfect model for Priests is Christ, and a sanctity that does not follow in his footsteps is worthless. Finally, a priest that does not constantly love Mary, the Mother of Christ, is inconceivable. There is none closer to Christ than She.

Teacher of Virtues

The blessed servant of God was called "teacher" in his last years; this nickname shows how much and with what regard and esteem his contemporaries and those subsequent held for him. And with just cause, for his virtue shined in a faith without obscurity, in a diligent and ardent love for our Great God; in poverty, scarcity and necessity; in the cross and penance; in the admirable and serious aspiration to serve the Church, which, like Paul, he desired with all the ardor of his soul be "with no spot or wrinkle" (Eph 5:27).

With such prudence, he deals with the matters for which St. Francis de Sales, Peter Bérulle, St. John Eudes, St. Vincent de Paul, St. Alfonsus Marie de Ligouri, St. Anthony Marie Claret, and many others have exhibited praises and from which they have reaped many fruits. We cannot overlook his commentaries, exposed with firm doctrine and solid reasoning, which flowed throughout the body of the Holy church by means of the orientations and decrees of the Sacred Tridentine Council.

3.

Following the Death of Saint John of Avila

Beatification, 15th of April of 1894

It is now time to consider the second part of blessed John's life, which began after his death. It cannot be said that one, whose fame of virtue spread throughout, who was so greatly esteemed and through whom God performed miraculous deeds, died absolutely. For these reasons, the accustomed processes began in the Archdiocese of Toledo. In 1759, Clement XIII, our predecessor, approved the Decree on his heroic virtues. And in the year 1894, on the fifteen of April, his name was solemnly inscribed into the Catalogue of the Blessed by Leo XIII.

Towards the equipollent canonization

Spread throughout the world, the news of his beatification so much attracted the admiration of all that it was thought that the Church should occupy herself with the investigation and confirmation of his sanctity. Because of this, the Cardinal Priests of the Sacred Congregation of Rites gathered together in order to consider the reopening of his cause, and on the 14th of March of 1952, they responded "affirmatively," "if it seemed fitting to the Holy Father".

In the request presented to this Holy See, the promoters were inclined to go through a process called equipollent rather than follow the more common process. We believed to be working correctly by following these desires. The use and customs of our ancestors and the norms of our Supreme Pontiffs justify this way of process. Although its use in the Church was not frequented, we could legitimately employ it as long as his heroic virtues and continuous veneration were unequivocally manifested. In the case of Blessed John of Avila, both of these things are manifested without a doubt.

Heroic virtues and uninterrupted cult

His detachment from his goods and their distribution to the poor; overcoming terrible accusations and jail without complaint; preaching and confessing incessantly; wandering from one place to another with a spirit of joy in order to gain souls for God; finally, to die as a victim: these things are not only indicators but also solid proofs of his sanctity.

If one investigates about his cult, it is also appears clear and ascertained. Once Blessed John died, the townspeople, the clergy and even the Saints themselves greatly venerated him, particularly from the time of his beatification and proclamation as patron of the Spanish Clergy by Pius XII, our predecessor of joyful remembrance, in the year 1946.

The last stage

In this way, on December 2nd of last year, the General Promoter of the Faith came to conclude that the cause of Blessed John of Avila deserved the honor of the Saints, and that nothing could oppose it.

Since the same opinion was held by the Sacred Congregation for the Cause of the Saints, whose meeting took place on the 10th of last February and by the President Cardinal Priests of the same congregation whose plenary council took place on the 24th of March, we have decided with great joy to concede to the equipollent canonization of Blessed John of Avila.

31st of May of 1970, Solemn canonization

This very day, with God's help, we have presided at these ceremonies with immense joy both on our behalf and of the Christian nation. In St. Peter's Basilica, occupied by a crowd of faithful coming from everywhere, specially from Spain, in the presence of many Cardinals of the Holy Church and Bishops of the Roman Curia of the Catholic Church, we are determined to accede to the pleadings of our venerable brother, the Cardinal Pablo Bertoli, Prefect of the Sacred Congregation for the Causes of the Saints, asking us to declare Blessed John of Avila a Saint.

Afterwards, Father Purpurado spoke briefly on the life, works and sanctity of the Blessed man; after we implored the intercession of the saints so that they may bring us the help and light of the Omnipotent God, as Supreme Master of the Church, we have declared the following, "For the honor of the Holy and Undivided Trinity, for the elevation of the Catholic Faith and the increase of Christian life, with the authority of Our Lord Jesus Christ, of the Blessed Apostles Peter and Paul and our own, after great consideration and imploring Divine help, we declare and define that Blessed John of Avila is a Saint. In the name of the Father, and of the Son, and of the Holy Spirit. Amen."

Once these words were pronounced at the plea of the Cardinal himself, we decreed that the now proclaimed Saint be inscribed into the Catalogue of the Saints and that the Decretal letters be drawn up as is the custom.

After attributing to the Omnipotent God the graces given to one with all those present, we had a homily on the admirable virtues and works of the new Saint, and we were the first to invoke his patrimony by celebrating the divine Sacrifice with a solemn rite at the High Altar of the Basilica.

With due investigation and reflection, all the facts that we have mentioned above, we manifest to the Universal Church. We order that to the complete or partial transcriptions of these apostolic letters, still in press, be given the same faith as the original so that they take the signature and seal of a notary.

Given in Rome united with Saint Peter, the 31st of May in the year of Our Lord, 1970, seventh year of our Pontificate.

Canonization of Blessed John of Avila

✠

Homily of the Holy Father Paul VI
Sunday 31st of May, 1970

Venerable brothers and beloved friends:

Let us give thanks to God that, along with the exaltation of Blessed John of Avila to the splendor of sanctity, He offers the universal Church an invitation to the study, imitation, type of worship, and invocation of a great priestly figure.

Let us praise the Spanish Episcopate, who, unsatisfied with Blessed John of Avila being proclaimed as the special protector of the diocesan clergy of Spain, as our predecessor of venerable remembrance, Pius XII, had done in his favor, has requested from this Apostolic See his canonization. We found as much in our Sacred Congregation for the causes of the saints as in our very person, the best and worthy dispositions for a celebrative act of such importance. May the Lord wish that this elevation of Blessed John of Avila to the catalog of the saints, in the glorious lines of the sons of the Celestial Church, serve to obtain for the Pilgrim Church on earth a new and powerful intercessor, a teacher of the spiritual life who is wise and benevolent, and an exemplary renovator of the ecclesiastical life and of Christian customs.

This, our desire, seems satisfied with making a historical comparison of the times in which the saint lived and worked with our times; comparison of two time periods that are certainly very diverse in themselves, but that alternatively appear analogous, not so much in deeds as in some inspiring beginnings, those of the human vicissitude of that time and those of today—for example, the awakening of vital energies and crises of ideas, a proper phenomenon of the 16th century as well as the 20th—times of reform and of conciliar debates as we are living now. Likewise, it appears providential in our day to invoke the figure of the Teacher of Avila due to the characteristic features of his priestly life, which give this Saint a particular worth and make him exceptionally appreciated by his contemporaries.

Saint John of Avila is a priest who, in many ways, can be called modern, especially because of the plurality of facets that his life brings to our consideration, and for the most part, for our imitation. Not in vain has he been presented to the Spanish clergy as their exemplary model and celestial Patron. We believe that he can be honored as a polyvalent figure for the priests of our times, in which it is said that the priesthood itself suffers a profound crisis—"crisis of identity"—as if the nature and mission of the priest no longer have sufficient motives to justify its presence in a society like ours, secularized and robbed of its sacredness. Every priest that doubts his own vocation can approach our Saint and obtain a reassuring response. In the same way, every scholar inclined to diminish the persona of the priest under the guise of a profane and utilitarian sociology would then, after observing John of Avila, find himself obliged to modify his restrictive and negative judgments about the priest's function in the modern world.

John is a poor and modest man on account of his own free will. He is not even supported by the insertion into the operative frames of the canonical system; he is not a Pastor; he is not a religious. He is a simple priest of scarce health and of even scarcer fortune after the first experiences of his ministry; he immediately suffers the most bitter trial that can be imposed on a faithful and fervent apostle—that of a process with its relative detention—due to suspected heresy, as was the custom of the time. He doesn't even get the chance to defend himself, embracing the great ideal of adventure. He had wanted to go as a missionary to the Americas, the Western "Indies", recently discovered at that time, but wasn't given the permission.

Still, John doesn't doubt. He is aware of his vocation. He has faith in his choice to become a priest. A psychological introspection of his biography would lead us to particularize in this certainty of his priestly "identity", which is the font of his serene zeal, of his apostolic fruitfulness, of the wisdom that made him a lucid reformer of ecclesiastical life and an exquisite director of consciences. Saint John of Avila teaches this at the very least, and this above all, to the cleric of our time to not doubt himself: he is the priest of Christ, minister of the Church, guide of his brothers.

He strongly brings attention to what today some priests and many seminarians don't consider a corroborating duty or a specific title received from the Church who qualifies their ministry; its proper definition—which can be called sociological—results from being a slave of Jesus Christ, who, as St. Paul would say about himself, is "set apart for the Gospel of God" (Rm1:1). This being set apart, this specification, which is furthermore that of a distinct and indispensable organ benefiting an entire living body (cf. 1Cor 12:16 ff), is today the first characteristic of the Catholic priesthood that is discussed and even debated for motives, often noble in themselves and, in some way, admissible. However when these motives tend to nullify being "set part", to assimilate the ecclesiastical state to that of the laity and to that which is profane and to justify the experience of a worldly life with the pretext that he should not be less than any other man, they then easily lead the called off his path, make of the priest an ordinary man, a salt lacking flavor, someone incapable of interior sacrifice and lacking the power to make judgments, to preach and be an example, things that are proper to a strong, pure and free follower of Christ. The sharp and demanding Word of the Lord, "Once the hand is laid on the plough, no one who looks back is fit for the kingdom of God" (Lk 9:62), had so profoundly penetrated this exemplary priest that in the complete giving of himself to Christ, he found his energy magnified.

His preaching became powerful and resulted renovating. Today, Saint John of Avila can still be a teacher of preachers, all the more worthy of being listened to and imitated, the less indulgent he was with artificial orators and writers of his time, and the more he abounded in wisdom, which was conceived in biblical and patristic sources. His personality grows and manifests itself in the ministry of preaching. Moreover, what seems to be contrary to the effort of public and exterior language, Avila also understood the practice of personal and interior language, proper to the ministry of the sacrament of penance and spiritual direction. And perhaps in this patient and silent ministry, extremely delicate and prudent, does his personality standout even more than in that of preaching.

The name of John of Avila is linked to his most significant work, the renowned work *Audi, filia* which is the book of interior teaching, full of religiosity, of Christian experience, and of human benevolence. It precedes the *Filotea*, which, in a certain sense, is an analogous work of another saint, Francis de Sales; it also precedes another whole set of literature of religious books, from the Council of Trent until our times, that will give depth and sincerity to catholic spiritual formation. Even in this, Avila is an exemplary teacher.

Oh how many more virtues can we recall for our edification! Avila was a productive writer. The aspect that also brings him closer to us in an admirable way and that offers us his dialogue is that of a saint.

Also the aspect of his acts edifies us. His acts were varied and tireless: correspondence, animating spiritual groups, especially those of priests, foundations of colleges for both clergy and youth, the conversion of great souls, like those of Luis of Granada, his disciple and biographer, and of future saints like John of God and Frances of Borja, and building friendships with the great spirits of his time, like Saint Ignatius and Saint Teresa. He truly is a great figure.

However, the place where we particularly want to place our attention is in the character of Avila as reformer, or better yet, as innovator, which is proper to St. John of Avila. Having lived during the period of transition, full of debates and controversies that preceded the Council of Trent, and even during and after the long and great Council, the Saint couldn't exempt himself from taking a stance before this great event. He couldn't personally take part because of his precarious health, but his is the well known Memorial titled *Reform of the Ecclesiastic State*[t] (1551), which the Archbishop of Granada, Pedro Guerrero, would make his own at the Council of Trent with general applause.

In the same way, other writings like: *Causes y remedies of Heresies*[u] (Second Memorial, 1561), show with what intensity and with what designs John of Avila participated in this historic event: of the same clear diagnosis of the gravity of evils that afflicted the Church of that time, loyalty, love, and hope are made translucent. Plus, what evangelical sincerity and filial devotion, what fidelity to tradition and confidence in the original and intrinsic constitution of the Church, and what primordial importance reserved for the true faith in order to heal evils and to foresee the renewal of the Church does he display when he addresses the Pope and the Pastors of the Church!

"John of Avila has been, in regards to reform, as well as in other spiritual areas, a precursor; the Council of Trent has adopted decisions that he had foreseen much earlier" (S. Charprenet, p.56).

But he wasn't a critical debater, as is said nowadays. He has been such an ardent and luminous soul that, to the renunciation of evil and to the suggestions of canonical remedies, he has added a school of intense spirituality (the study of Sacred Scripture, the practice of mental prayer, the imitation of Christ and the translation of such a book into Spanish, adoration of the Eucharist, devotion to the Blessed Virgin Mary, defense of sacred celibacy, love for the church even when one of its members was too severe with him…), and he has been the first to practice the teachings of his own school.

We repeat that, he's a great model for the daughter and glory of the land of Spain, as for the Catholic Spain that is trained to drastically live her faith, causing from the bosom of her moral and

---

[t] *Reformación del Estado Eclesiástico (1551)*
[u] *Causas y remedios de las herejías (Memorial Segundo, 1561)*

spiritual traditions, little by little, in those critical moments of her history, the emergence of the hero, the wise, the Saint.

May this Saint, who we are happy to exalt before the Church, be her favorable intercessor for the graces that the Church evidently needs now more than ever: firmness in the true faith, authentic love for the Church, the holiness of her clergy, fidelity to the Council, and the imitation of Christ as it should be in these modern times. And may his prophetic figure, crowned today with the halo of sanctity, pour out the truth, love, and peace of Christ upon the earth.

NOTES

[1] De informat. Episcop. Or De dignitate sacerdotali (ML 139,170).
[2] Letter to the Eph 13; MG 5,745
[3] De informat. Episcop. ML 139,170
[4] *Quis loquetur potentias Domini auditas faciet omens laudes eius?*
[5] *Venite et videte opera Dei, benignissimi, et dulcissimi super sacerdotes*
[6] St. Greg. Dialog 1.4, c. 58: ML 77, 425-28.
[7] St. Greg. Dialog 1.4, c. 58: ML 77, 425-28)
[8] *Ipsi gloria in saecula saeculorum*
[9] *Gerberto (afterwards Sylvester II), De informat. Episcop., o.p. attributed to St. Ambrose; ML 139, 17.*
[10] De considerat. 1.2 c.7 (ML 182,750), n. 164: *monstruosa res gradus summus, et animus infimus; sedes prima et vita ima.*
[11] Lev 21:6; Mass of Corpus Christi
[12] *Munus absconditum extinguit iras.*
[13] *De sacerdot.* 1,6,4: MG 48,680-81.
[14] *De paenit.* 1.2c10,92: ML 16,540. *Talium, Domine, preces numquam spernis, si, ut pro me orent, ipse inspiraveris.*
[15] *De diligendo Deo* c. 7,22: ML 182,987. *Tepida est omnis oratio, quam no praecedit inspiratio.*
[16] *Comm. in Mal.* 1.8: ML 77, 428.
[17] In the 16th century, Paul was considered the author of Hebrews.
[18] St. Gregory the Great, *Dialog.* 1.4 c.59: ML 77,428.
[19] Pseudo-Ambrose, *Precat.in prep. ad Missam* 2: ML, 830s.
[20] *Tract. De charitat.* C.7,31.32: ML 184,599-600.
[21] *Sermo contra Auxentium. De basilicas tradendis* 2: ML 16, 1050. *Adversus arma, milites, Gothos quoque, lacrymae meae arma sunt; talia enim munimenta sunt sacerdotis.*
[22] *In Lev. Homil.* 5,3,4: MG 12, 452-54.
[23] *De officiis* 1.4: ML 16,34. *Neque enim minus vos diligo quos sub Evangelio genui, quam si coniugio suscepissem.*
[24] *De sacerdot.* 1.6,4: MG 48,68. The priest must act *ac si omnium pater sit.*
[25] *Reg. pastor. p.1. c. 10:*ML 77,23f.
[26] *Epist.* 60,17: ML 22,601.
[27] *Reg. pastor. p. 1. c. 10:* ML 77,23f.

²⁸ Pseudo-Dionysius, *De eccles. hierarch.* c. 1,3: MG 3,374. *Sicut enim qui sacrum ordinem nominavit, omnium simul compendio sacrorum dixit dispensationem; ita qui summum sacerdotem appellat, Deo intime unitum ad divinum plane virum significant.*

²⁹ Pseudo-Jerome, *Epist.* 1, *Virginitatis laus* 16; ML 30, 181. *Ita ergo, per te, quasi per vivam hostiam sanctificentur ceterae, cum quibus te ita in omnibus exhibeas, ut quisquis vitam tuam aut visu aut auditu contingat, sanctificationis vim sentiat.*

³⁰ *Homil. 17 in Evang.* 16; ML 76, 1147.

³¹ Ex 28:42: *femoralia, ut operiret turpitudinem suam.*

³² *Ille me clarificabit, quia de me accipiet.*

³³ *Ille testimonium perhibebit de me.*

³⁴ *De sacerdot.* 1.6,4: MG 48,681. "Itaque sic differre debet omnibus precator, virtutis minentia, quantum praecellit et ipso distat officio; cumque et Spiritum Sanctum advocaverit, et reverendam illam immolaverit hostiam..., ubi illum, dic mihi, nostra aestimatione ponemus? Quantum ab illo splendorem poscemus et quantam religionem...? Expende nunc, quales oporteat esse manus eius, tantarum rerum ministras, qualem linguam Christum illa fundentem, aut quo igne mundiorem et sanctiorem animam eius!..."

"Tunc enim ey Angeli circundant sacerdotem, et Tribunal, atque altaris locus caelestibus virtutibus adimpletur, in honorem illius qui immolatur; quod quidem ex ipsis quae aguntur ostenditur. Ego audivi, referente aliquo, quod presbyter quidam vitae sanctitate mirabilis, et qui revelationes soleret videre, retulisset illi tale spectaculum se aliquando vidisse, sancti sacrificii tempore, et conspexisse angelorum multitudinem (sicut possibile erat intueri) stolis fulgentibus, et altare coronatum cum officio quo circa regem suum milites stare consueverunt; quod mihi quidem facile persuasum est".

"Alter vero mihi retulit ab alio se audisse, quod de saeculo hoc recedentes, qui participes mysteriorum illorom in continetia munda fuerint, cum effaverint ultimum spiritum, subiici alacres manibus Angelorum. Necdum ergo inhorrescis, quod ad tale ministerium, me innitebaris inducere, indutum sordibus et vitiis; sacerdotum inserere dignitati, quem talem Christus a convivantium congregatione separaverit? Splendore igitur vitae totum illuminantis orbem fulgere debet anima sacerdotis; nostra autem tantis tenebris operitur male et curvatur semper ut nec ad Deum suum cum fiducia audeat aliquando respicere. Sacerdotes sal terrae sunt; nostram autem insipientiam, aut in omnibus ignorantiam, quis queat facile sustinere, exceptis vobis, qui nimium nos diligere decrevistis?"

³⁵ "Si enim Angeli, Te adorantes et laudantes, tremunt mira exultatione replete, ego peccator dum Tibi assisto, laudes dico, sacrificium offero, cur non corde paveo, vultu palleo, labiis tremo, toto corpora inhorresco? Sic iam obortis lacrymis coran Te indesinenter lugeo... Vehemen-

ter admoror, dum Te nimis Terribilem oculis fidei cerno. Miserum me, quando sic induruit cor meum! Et oculi mei indesinenter non producunt flumin lacrymarum, dum servus sermocinatur coram Domino suo, homo cum Deo, et creatura cum Creatore; qui factus est ex limo cum eo qui omnia fecit ex nihilo".

"Dator omnium bonorum Deus, da mihi inter laudes tuas fontem lacrymarum, simul cum cordis puritate et mentis iubilatione, ut perfecte diligens, et digne Te laudans, ipso Cordis palato sentiam, gustem et sapiam quam dulcis et suavis es, Domine".

36 Pseudo-Ambrose, *Precat. 2 in praep. ad Missam* 1: ML 17, 830-42. "Doce me servum tuum indignum, qui inter cetera dona tua ad officium sacerdotale vocare dignatus es, nullis meis meritis, sed sola dignationes misericordiae Tuae: doce me, quaeso, per Spiritum, tantum mysterium tractare ea reverentia et honore, eaque vocatione et timore quo oportet: fac me, Domine Jesu-Christe, per gratiam tuam, semper illud de tanto mysterio et cogitare, quod Tibi placet et expedit animae mea"

"Quanta enim, Domine Jesu-Christe, cordis contritione et lacrymarum fonte, quanta reverentia et tremore, quanta corporis castitate et animae puritate, illud divinum et caeleste sacrificium est celebrandum, abi caro tua in veritate sumitur, ubi sanguis tuus in veritate bibitur"

"quis dignus erit..., nisi tu ipse feceris dignum? Scio, et vere scio, et ipsi Veritati tuae confiteor, quia non sum dignus accedere ad ministerium tuum propter nimia peccata mea et infinitas negligentias meas"

37 *Epist.* 125, 16: ML 22m 1082. "Ita ergo age, et vive in monasterio, ut clericua esse merearis, et adolescentiam tuam nulla sorde commacules, ut ad altare Christi quasi de thalamo virgo procedas".

38 *Dialog.* 1.4 c. 59: ML 77,428.
39 *Ecce sponsus venit, exite obviam ei.*
40 *Ego a Te debeo baptizari, et Tu venis ad me?*
41 *Exi a me, Domine, quoniam homo peccator sum.*
42 *Pactum meum fuit cum Levi vitae et pacis; et dedi ei timorem, et timuit me, et a facie nominis mei pavebat.*
43 *Amice, quomodo huc intrasti non habens vestem nuptialem?*
44 Pseudo-Dionysius, *De ecles. Hierarch.* c.3,9-10: MG 3,438-39. *eos qui ad Sacramenta caelestia conficienda procedunt, ea oportet esse munditia, ut ipsas animae extremas imagines purgatas habeant; sicque ad reverenda mysteria, quantum fas es, similitudine puritatis accedere. consequitur supremam munditiem, ut in castissimo habitu divinae spei constitutus, ad sequentia quoque divina bonitatis imagine prodeat, vinculis omnibus mortalis affectionis liber ac expeditus, et qui in unius transierit spem.*
45 Pseudo-Dionysius, *De ecles. hierarch.* c.3,5: MG 3,444.
46 *Ecce manus tradentis me mecum est in mensa.*
47 *In Lc. Ev. Expositio* 1.6 c. 22, ML 92,597-98.
48 *Juda, osculo filium hominis tradis?*

⁴⁹ *qui loquuntur pacem cum proximo suo, mala autem in cordibus eorum?*

⁵⁰ *Quid tibi cum feminis qui ad altare confabularis cum Christo?*

⁵¹ *Audent agni immaculati sacras contingere carnes, et intingere in sanguinem Salvatoris manus nefarias, quae paulo ante carnes (proh dolor) meretricias attectaverunt. Declam. Ex S. Bernardo* 12: ML 184,444.

⁵² *Aperuerunt super me os sum, sicut leo rapiens et rugiens*

⁵³ *. . . sed est qui quaerat et judicet.*

⁵⁴ *Deus, ne tacueris, quia os peccatoris et os dolosi super me apertum est*

⁵⁵ *. . . et sicut parturiens*

⁵⁶ *De Trin.* 4,14: ML 42, 899-901; *In Ps* 21:27-28; ML 36,179' *Epist.* 76,1: ML 33, 264.

⁵⁷. Ibid.

⁵⁸ Pseudo-Chrysostom, *Opus imperfectum, In Mt homil.* 40,28 MG 56,85. *Laici, si peccant, facile emendatur; clerici, si delinquunt, inemendables evadunt.*

⁵⁹ *Irritam quis faciens legem Moysis, duobus vel tribgus testibus, sine miseratione moritur. Quanto majis putatis deteriora mereri supplicia, qui filium Dei conculcaverit, et sanguinem testamenti, in quo sanctificatus est, pollutum duxerit, et spiritui gratiae contumeliam fecerit? Scimus enim, qui dixit: Mihi vindicta, et ego retriuam; et iterum: Iudicabit Dominus populum suum.... Horrendum est incidere in manus Dei viventis!*

⁶⁰ *Caeleste tenet officium, angelus Domini exercituum factus est; tanquam angelus aut eligitur, aut reprobatur. Inventa in angelis pravitate, et districtius iudicetur necesse est, et inexorabilior quam humana Declamat. ex S. Bernardo* 21 n. 24: ML 184.

⁶¹ *Ibid.* n. 25. *Quo progrederis? An ut ab altiori gradu sit casus gravior? Nec enim sic paulatim decidas, sed tanquam fulgur in impetu vehementi; quasi alter Satanas, subito deiicieris*

⁶² *Qui peccat sine timore et paenitentia, et qui indigne communicat.*

⁶³ *Non est qui vicem meam doleat.*

⁶⁴ *...numquid super his continebis te, Domine? Tacebis, et affliges nos vehementer?*

⁶⁵ *Filius stultus moestitia matris suae.*

⁶⁶ *In ep. ad Tit.* 1,6: ML 26,598.

⁶⁷ *De sacerdotio* 1.3 and 6: MG 48, 639-660.677-692}

⁶⁸ *Epist.classis* I epist. 21,1s: ML 33,88.

⁶⁹ *Reg. pastor.* p.1. c. 10: ML 77,23; p. 2. c.3.7: ML 77,28.40.

⁷⁰ *De sacerdot.* 1.3,6: MG 48643.

⁷¹ *Despondi enim vos uni viro, virginem castam exhibere Christo*

⁷² *Ars artium, regimen animarum (Regul. pastor.* p.1. c.1:ML 77,14).

⁷³ Cf. Ez 3:9. St. John of Avila confuses Jeremiah with Ezekiel.

⁷⁴ *Repletus sum fortitudine Domini, ut annuntiem Iacob scelus suum.*

⁷⁵ Pseudo-Dionisio, *De eccl. hierarch.* 5,4.6.7: MG 3,504 and 507.

⁷⁶ Pseudo-Clemente, *Epist.* 1 Clementis *ad Iacobum fratrem Domini*: ML 130, 19-38; Epist. 3 *Clementis Papae*: ML 130,43-54.

⁷⁷ *Seniores qui in vobis sunt…*
⁷⁸ *hi quibus adhuc aliena auxilia necessaria sunt, ad subveniendum aliis promovendi non sunt* Cf. St. Gregory the Great, *Epist.* 1.1 *epist.* 25: ML 77, 468].
⁷⁹ *Eligere studeant personas sufficientes, idoneas, vita probatas, discretas, modestas atque peritas, ad tam salubre ministerium atque officium exequendum* (C.7 III 6 in Clem.).
⁸⁰ *Magnum sacramentum est animae suscitatio* (St. Bernard, *Epist.* 113,4: ML 182,258; *Medit. de humana condit.* C.2,8: ML 184,490).
⁸¹ *Curabant cum ignominia contritionem filiae populi mei, dicentes: Pax, pax, et non erat pax.*
⁸² *…confortant manus pessimorum.*
⁸³ Conc. Trid., ses. 23 c.14 *de ref.*
⁸⁴ *Ibid.* c. 15.
⁸⁵ *Plantatio Domini ad glorificandum.*
⁸⁶ *Populum istum creavi mihi; laudem meam narrabit.*

NOTES

Notes